Longman Science 11–13 Series
General Editor: John L. Lewis O.B.E.

Also in this series:
Biology 11–13
Chemistry 11–13
Physics 11–13

ELECTRONICS 11–13

G. E. Foxcroft O.B.E.
Formerly Senior Science Master, Rugby School

J. L. Lewis O.B.E., F.Inst.P.
Formerly Senior Science Master, Malvern College

M. K. Summers
Oxford University Department of Educational Studies

Longman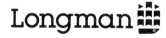

LONGMAN GROUP LIMITED
Longman House, Burnt Mill, Harlow, Essex CM20 2JE, England
and Associated Companies throughout the World

© Longman Group Limited 1986

First published 1986
ISBN 0 582 31112 8

Set in 11 on 12 pt Univers light

Printed in Great Britain
by Mackays of Chatham Limited.

Contents

Acknowledgements

We are grateful to the following for permission to reproduce photographs:
Barclays Bank, page 35; Crown copyright, reproduced with the permission of the Controller of Her Majesty's Stationery Office, page 89; IBM, page 90.
All other photographs taken by Longman Photographic Unit (digital ammeter and voltmeter lent by Griffin and George).

Cover photograph depicts the Valiant Turtle remote control robot, courtesy of Valiant Designs, London SW11 4NB (01-720-3947).

Preface

The earlier book in this series, *Physics 11-13*, used a modern experimental approach to impart an understanding of the principles of physics. This book attempts to do the same. Since *Physics 11-13* was written, it has become increasingly clear that some electronics should be incorporated into such a physics course, because electronics has become an important part of modern physics and pupils should be introduced, even if only at an elementary level, to something which will increasingly influence their lives.

It is suggested that electronics should be studied by all pupils and not be a separate course on its own. This book assumes therefore that electronics will be incorporated with the work on electricity which is part of all physics courses.

The electronics is based on that developed by the Independent Schools' Microelectronics Centre at Westminster College, Oxford. The authors are very grateful to the Management Committee of the Centre for their permission to reproduce ISMEC material here.

The temptation to include a large amount of electronics was resisted, even though this may disappoint some enthusiasts. The decision was made to concentrate on a few simple, but useful, devices, leading on to switching and to elementary work with logic. Some might have preferred a detailed treatment of the transistor, but transistors become increasingly obsolescent as new devices are introduced, as happened to thermionic valves. It is advocated here that a systems approach is adopted, since the systems do not change whatever the devices employed. Switching is the basis of all modern digital electronics and the emphasis has therefore been placed on it.

The electronics work advocated in this book has been tried in schools of various kinds, and the leading suppliers of school apparatus have produced kits of modules to cover the proposed work.

The authors are very grateful to Alec Porch, John Parkin and David Rogers who have helped them greatly in the preparation of the book.

Chapter 1 **Taking stock**

You have already studied some of the ways in which electric circuits behave. In this book we will be introducing you to some electronic devices, but in this chapter we will remind you of some of the things that you need to know about electric currents.

Experiment 1.1   Using a cell and a lamp
The photograph shows a lamp and a cell connected so that the lamp lights.

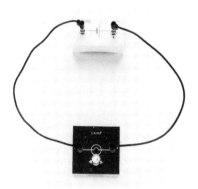

1. What happens if you put the cell the other way round in the circuit? Does it make any difference?

2. Does it make any difference if you put the lamp the other way round?

3. Does it make any difference to the brightness of the lamp whether you use long or short leads when connecting the circuit?

4. What happens if there is a gap in the circuit?

The electric circuit

Experiment 1.1 shows that it does not matter which way round you put the cell or the lamp as long as they are joined in a circuit. The lamp will not light if a gap is left. It is usual to speak about an electric current flowing round an electric circuit, but at this point it is not necessary to know what an electric current is, though you will learn later that it is a flow of charge.

Experiment 1.2   Using several lamps and several cells

1. If two lamps are joined in line as in the photograph below (left), they are said to be 'in series'. How does the brightness compare with the brightness produced when the cell was connected to only one lamp?

2. What happens to the brightness if two cells in series are connected across the two lamps as in the second photograph?

3. What happens to the brightness if one cell is across three lamps in series?

4. What happens to the brightness if there are three cells in series across one lamp?

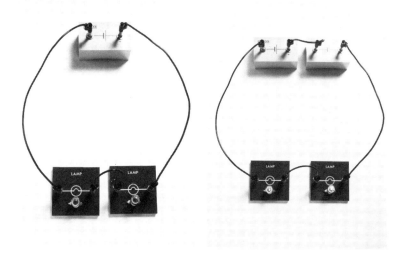

Brightness of lamps

Experiments show that the lamps glow with the same brightness if there is one cell across one lamp, two cells across two lamps or three cells across three lamps. We shall call this 'normal brightness'. If more cells are added, the lamps glow more brightly. With fewer cells, they would be less bright. This suggests that three cells drive the same current through three lamps in series, as two cells do through two lamps and as one cell does through one lamp. If the number of lamps is kept the same, adding more cells makes the current bigger.

Experiment 1.3 Conductors and insulators

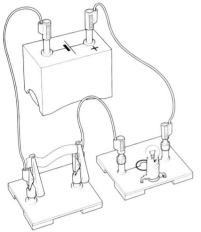

If there is an air gap in a circuit, no current flows. We say that air is an *insulator*. A strip of metal and the leads you have been using allow a current to flow: these are therefore called *conductors*.

1. The drawing shows a cell, a lamp and a piece of paper held between two crocodile clips, in series. Connect the circuit and find out if paper is a conductor or an insulator.

2. Collect as many different objects as you can and test each of them. Make a list showing which are conductors and which are insulators.

Experiment 1.4 Resistance wire

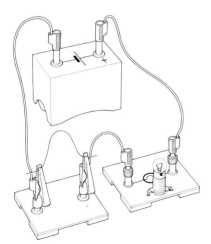

For this experiment you are provided with some special wire: eureka wire is the name for it, but there is no need to remember that.

1. Use the same apparatus as in Experiment 1.3. Put a very short length of the wire between the crocodile clips. Does the lamp light or not? Is the wire a conductor or an insulator?

2. Then try a longer piece of eureka wire between the crocodile clips. Is there any change in the brightness of the lamp?

3. Now try a very much longer piece of the wire. What happens to the lamp now? If your piece of wire is very long, see it does not touch part of itself. What happens if it does?

The dimmer

The previous experiment has shown that when a short length of eureka wire is used, the lamp glows brightly. But when a longer and longer piece is used, it is harder for current to flow and the lamp becomes dimmer. A long wire offers more resistance than a short wire, and so less current flows. For that reason such wire is called *resistance wire*.

With a short length of resistance wire in the circuit, the lamp is bright. With a long piece the lamp is dim. This suggests that a length of such wire included in a circuit would make a good *dimmer* for changing the brightness of lamps. But a long piece of wire would be inconvenient, so manufacturers wind it up into a convenient coil with a sliding contact and a control knob on top to turn it. This varies the length of the part of the wire through which the current flows.

A piece of wire or other substance which offers some resistance to a current is called a *resistor*. A dimmer is called a *variable resistor* and another name sometimes used for it is a *rheostat*.

Experiment 1.5   The dimmer

1. Connect two cells and a lamp in series so that the lamp glows brightly.

2. Insert a dimmer in the circuit so that you can control the brightness of the lamp. Does it make any difference which side of the lamp you put the dimmer?

Measuring current

Current is measured with a meter called an *ammeter*. An ammeter has to be connected in a circuit so that the current to be measured passes through it. The unit in which current is measured is called the *ampere*. When writing down the size of a current, it may be written as 0.3 ampere or 0.3 A.

An ammeter has to be connected in a circuit the right way round. To help you to do this, one of its terminals is coloured

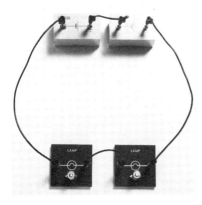

red (or marked +) and the other black (or marked −). It should be connected so that the current, flowing from the positive terminal of the cell (the small central button of the cell), enters the meter through the red terminal.

Experiment 1.6 Lamps in series

We have already said that when lamps are arranged in line, as in the photograph on the left, they are said to be in series.

1. Put two lamps in series with two cells. The lamps should glow with normal brightness.

2. Connect an ammeter in the circuit between the lamps and measure the current.

3. Measure the current between the cells and the lamps. Also measure it between the cells. What do you notice?

4. Measure the current in a series circuit made from one cell and two lamps.

In a series circuit, the current is the same all round the circuit. Reducing the number of cells results in a smaller current so the lamps are not as bright as normal.

Experiment 1.7 Lamps in parallel

When lamps are arranged as on the left, they are said to be 'in parallel'. The lamps are placed side by side and joined at each end.

1. Put two lamps in parallel with one cell across the ends. The lamps should glow with normal brightness.

2. Connect an ammeter in the circuit to measure the current from the cell. Make a note of the current.

3. Now measure the current passing through each lamp and write down the values. What do you notice about these values and the size of the current from the cell?

4. Try using a dimmer in place of one of the lamps.

In a parallel circuit, the current flowing from the cell is equal to the total of the currents in the parallel branches.

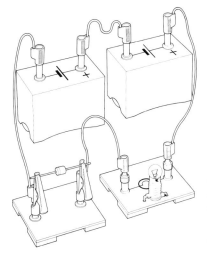

Experiment 1.8 The diode

1. Connect two cells, a lamp and a diode held between two crocodile clips in series as shown.

2. What happens to the lamp?

3. Turn the cells round. What happens to the lamp this time?

4. Now turn the diode round. What happens?

5. Measure the current in the circuit when the lamp is glowing and when it is not glowing.

The diode is a little device which has a low resistance to current flowing one way and a very high resistance to current flowing the other way. In effect it allows current to travel through it in one direction but not the other.

Sometimes it is called a *rectifier*, but the more usual name for it is a *diode*. We shall call it a diode in this book.

Circuit diagrams

To draw a picture of three lamps in parallel across two cells would be a very awkward business if it had to be drawn like some of those previously. For this reason scientists draw electric circuits with diagrams using special signs and symbols.

The symbol for a cell is two parallel lines as shown below, one longer and thinner than the other. We have already seen that it matters which way round a cell is used in a circuit.

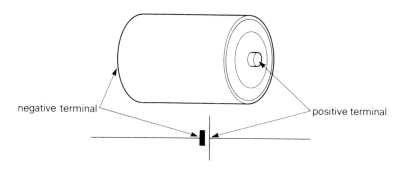

negative terminal   positive terminal

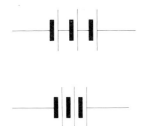

You will notice that the terminals of most cells are labelled + and −. With your cells, the central 'button' is the positive terminal and the metal base at the other end is the negative terminal. In the symbol for the cell, the long line represents the positive terminal, the short line the negative one.

When a number of cells (say, three) are connected in series (joined + to − in a line) to form a battery, this can be drawn in a circuit diagram in either of the ways shown on the left. Several cells in series are sometimes shown with dashes between two cells as below.

The standard symbol for a lamp is shown below on the left. Thus the circuit for one lamp and one cell would be drawn like this:

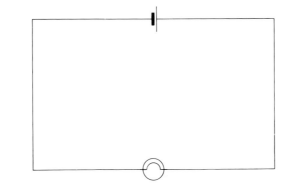

The straight lines represent the connecting leads. They are usually drawn straight, with right-angled corners, to make the diagrams neat and easy to follow. You have found in your experiments that it is necessary to have a complete circuit in order to get a lamp to light. A complete circuit must therefore be shown in the circuit diagram by joining with lines as was done above. Where leads are joined together, the junction is marked with a dot, as shown on the left.

A circuit with three lamps in parallel across two cells might be drawn in a number of different ways:

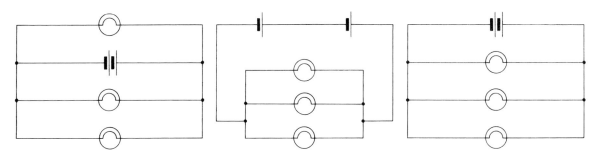

In a circuit diagram the symbol for a resistor was at one time a zig-zag line, but it is now more usual to use the rectangular symbol shown below.

The symbol for a variable resistor or rheostat is the same, but with an arrow through it.

Diodes are usually shown by the symbol below. The current flows easily in the direction of the arrowhead, but not the other way.

The symbol for an ammeter is this:

Background reading

A few thousand years ago information was passed from one person to another by word of mouth. The amount of information that a man could have was limited by his memory. Most people had to work very hard just to feed, clothe and house themselves. With the invention of writing and printing people were able to learn new ideas quickly. They learned better ways of growing crops and making tools. They eventually learned how to make machines which worked faster than humans. So fewer people were needed to produce more food and life became a little easier.

Today we have computers to run the machines for us. They also have large memories to store vast amounts of information and more and more people have access to this information. Microelectronics holds the promise of a better life for everyone, but we need to learn quickly how to control microelectronics before it controls us. The more we understand about what microelectronics can and cannot do, the more we shall be able to use this gift properly. This is just one of the arguments for giving microelectronics a place in everyone's education.

(From *Microelectronics: A Practical Introduction* by R. A. Sparkes, published by Hutchinson Education.)

1. How do you think people communicated before the days of written material?

2. You have heard about computers. In what ways do you think they make communication easier?

3. What does the author mean about computers controlling us?

4. What do you think might be the reasons for studying microelectronics in schools?

Chapter 2 **Questions**

In these questions, *normal brightness* means the brightness of a lamp when lit by one cell.

1. Draw a circuit diagram for each of the following:
a. one cell across two lamps and a resistor, all in series,
b. a battery of two cells across two lamps in parallel,
c. a circuit in which there is a current flowing from a battery through a diode, a rheostat and an ammeter in series.

2. Suppose you are given three similar lamps and one cell. Draw the circuit diagrams which would give each of the following results:
a. all three lamps glow dimly with the same brightness,
b. all three lamps glow with normal brightness,
c. two lamps glow equally dimly and one with normal brightness.
   What will happen if one lamp is unscrewed from its holder in b? In c, what will happen if one of the dimly lit lamps is unscrewed?

3. Look at these circuits carefully. For each circuit, do you think the lamp will glow brighter than normal, with normal brightness, dimly or not at all? Give a reason for your answer.

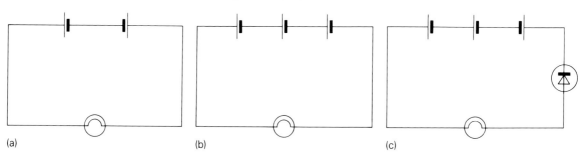

(a)   (b)   (c)

4. Two of the circuits below are the same electrically. One is different. Which is the different one?

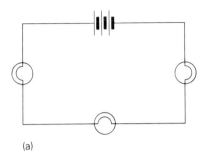

(a)

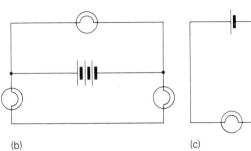

(b)

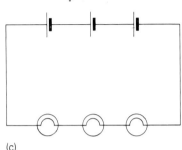

(c)

5. Are these circuits electrically the same or different? Do the ammeters read the same or differently?

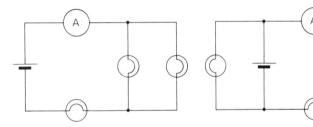

6. The resistors in these circuits are similar. Are the circuits electrically the same or different? Give a reason.

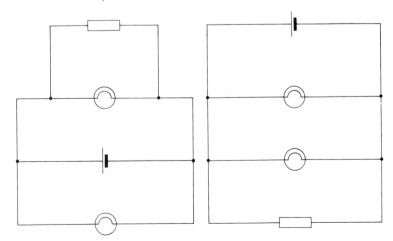

7. The following circuits include diodes. Which lamps (A, B, C, ...) will light?

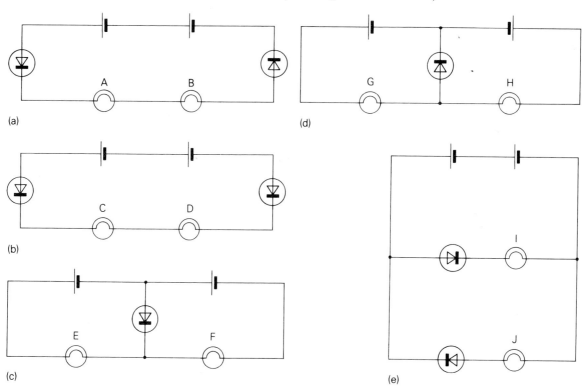

(a)

(b)

(c)

(d)

(e)

8. State which lamps (A, B, C, D) in the circuits below will have their brightness affected when the rheostats (X, Y, Z) are turned.

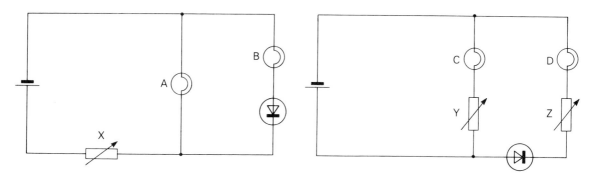

9. All the cells in the circuits below are similar, and all the lamps are similar. State whether each of the lamps will be extra bright, at normal brightness, dim or out.

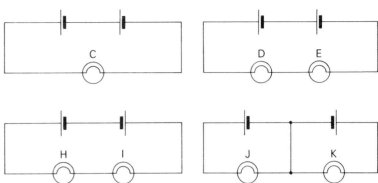

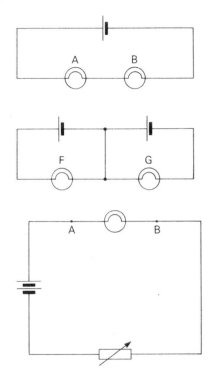

10. What would you expect to happen to the lamp in the circuit on the left:
a. if the resistance of the variable resistor is reduced,
b. if a piece of copper wire (a good conductor) is connected between the points A and B,
c. if a second, similar lamp is connected to the points A and B in parallel with the first lamp,
d. if one of the cells is turned round?

11. The circuit below shows three cells lighting three lamps.
a. The points X and Y are joined by a piece of copper wire (a good conductor). What will happen to the brightness of lamp A, and to the brightness of lamps B and C?
b. A variable resistor is now connected between X and Y in place of the copper wire. What do you think will happen to the brightness of the lamps as the variable resistor is turned?

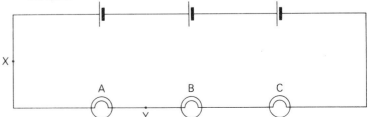

13

12. (Harder) In the circuit below, which lamps will glow more brightly than normal and which less brightly than normal?

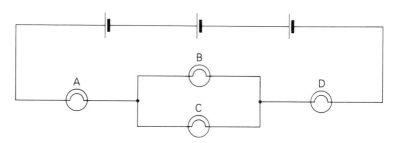

13. The battery X is used to light the two lamps P and Q. It is found that P glows more brightly than Q. Someone suggests this is 'because the current decreases as it moves round the circuit'. How would you test this suggestion (a) if you had a suitable ammeter, (b) if you had no other apparatus?

If you think the suggestion is incorrect, give a more likely explanation.

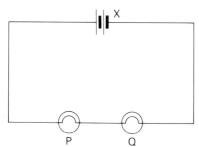

14. For each of the following circuits, describe how the brightness of the lamps changes as the resistance of the rheostat is reduced.

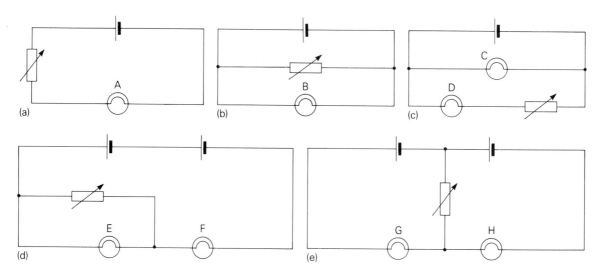

14

terminals   lamps

○ A

○ B   X

○ C

○ D   Y

15. A closed box has four terminals, A, B, C and D, and two similar lamps, X and Y, screwed into sockets in it.

When a cell is connected to terminals A and D, lamp X lights normally. When the cell is connected to A and C, nothing happens until B and D are connected by a piece of copper wire when both lamps light dimly.

a. Draw a diagram to show the connections inside the box.

b. How would you connect the cell to make lamp Y light normally without lamp X lighting?

c. How would you get both lamps to light brightly?

16. Two one-way streets P and Q merge into another one-way street R.

a. If one car per minute travels along road P and four cars per minute along road R, how many cars per minute will travel along road Q?

road P

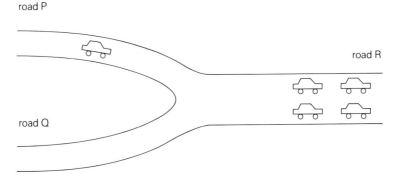

road R

road Q

b. There is a junction in an electric circuit. If 1 A flows along PR and 3 A along QR, what current will flow along RS?

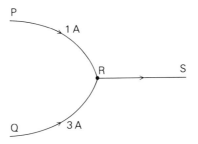

15

17. All the circuits below use similar cells and similar lamps. In figure (a) the current is 0.2 A. In each of the other circuits, say whether the current will be 0, between 0 and 0.2 A, 0.2 A or greater than 0.2 A. Give a reason for each answer.

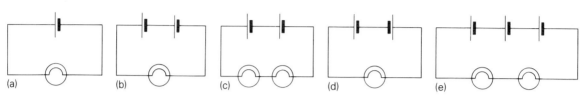

(a)   (b)   (c)   (d)   (e)

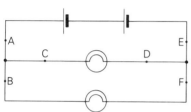

18. In the circuit on the left, the lamps are similar to each other. When an ammeter is placed at A, it reads 0.6 A.
a. What would be the reading if the ammeter were placed at B?
b. What would it read if placed at C, D, E and F?

19. In the circuit below, what are represented by the symbols labelled (a), (b), (c), (d) and (e)?
   If the current from the cells is 0.1 A and the lamps are all similar, what can you say about the current flowing through each of the lamps?

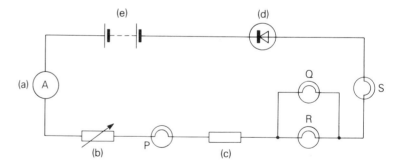

Chapter 3 # Some useful electronic components

In this chapter we shall consider some devices which play a part in modern electronics as well being useful to us in the later parts of this book.

The light emitting diode (LED)

The **L**ight **E**mitting **D**iode, or 'LED' as it is usually called for short, is an inexpensive device widely used in electronic circuits in order to show that a current is flowing. The circuit diagram symbol for an LED is this:

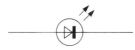

As an LED can be damaged if too big a current flows through it, the LED module has a resistor in series with the LED and this prevents the current from getting too large. In all the circuit diagrams which follow, that resistor is always shown.

Experiment 3.1   The light emitting diode (LED)

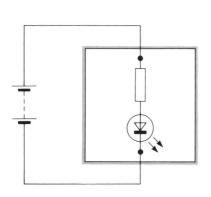

1. Connect an LED module and a battery as shown.

2. What happens to the LED when the circuit is connected?

3. Change round the connections to the LED module. What happens this time?

An LED will allow current to pass through it in only one direction. As with an ordinary diode, the arrowhead in the circuit diagram symbol points the way in which current can flow. But the LED differs from the ordinary diode since the passage of current through it causes light to be given out.

17

Experiment 3.2 Brightness and current

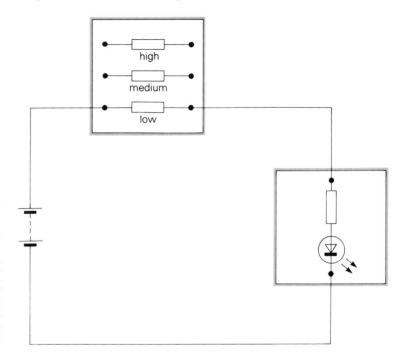

1. Connect the circuit shown above, using the LED module, the resistor module and a battery. The resistor module has separate connections so that the resistance can be high, medium or low. Use the low value first. Notice how brightly the LED glows.

2. Now use the medium resistance in place of the low one. What happens to the brightness of the LED?

3. Finally use the high resistance. What happens to the brightness this time?

4. As the resistance gets greater, so the current in the circuit gets less. How does the brightness of the LED depend on the current passing through it?

   The circuit diagram on the left shows how the arrangement above would normally be drawn.

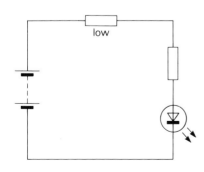

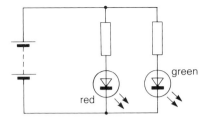

Experiment 3.3 LEDs in parallel

1. Set up the circuit shown using one red LED module, one green LED module and a battery. Why do both LEDs glow?

2. If another LED were connected in parallel with the above two, how brightly would you expect it to glow? Test your answer with another LED.

Positive and negative supply rails

Parallel connections are often used in electronic circuits, as you will find later in this book. The last experiment is a useful introduction to the idea of positive and negative supply rails, as shown in the diagram below.

If an LED is connected between the positive supply rail and the negative supply rail, a current will flow through it (assuming, of course, that it is connected the right way round).

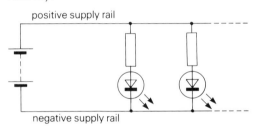

positive supply rail

negative supply rail

Project A current direction indicator

In this book we will suggest a number of projects from time to time which you may like to try to solve for yourself, though of course you can get advice from your teacher if necessary. However it is the normal job of an electronics engineer to solve problems and it is much more fun to do it on your own.

The problem here is to use a red LED module and a green LED module to construct a current direction indicator. It should be such that when the battery is connected one way round the green LED glows; and when the battery connections are the other way round the red LED glows.

The light dependent resistor (LDR) and the buzzer

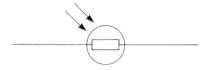

The circuit diagram symbol for a **L**ight **D**ependent **R**esistor, or 'LDR', is shown on the left.

Experiment 3.4 The light dependent resistor (LDR)

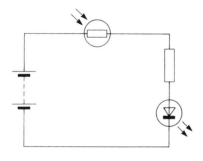

1. Set up the circuit shown on the left using a light dependent resistor module in series with an LED module and a battery.

2. What happens to the brightness of the LED when light is shone on the LDR? What happens when the LDR is covered up?

3. What does this tell you about the resistance of the LDR in the light and in the dark?

4. Does the circuit behave any differently if the connections to the LDR are changed round?

The experiment shows that current will flow in either direction through the LDR, as with an ordinary resistor. However, when it is dark, the LDR has a high resistance and therefore allows little current to pass. In bright light, the LDR's resistance falls to a low value and a much bigger current can flow.

Experiment 3.5   The buzzer

There is a buzzer module amongst the electronics modules and it makes a sound when an electric current passes through it. In circuit diagrams it will be represented by this symbol:

1. Set up the circuit shown below using the buzzer module, the resistor module and the battery.

2. Investigate whether it makes any difference which way round the buzzer is connected in the circuit.

3. Replace the low value resistor with the medium and then the high value resistors. What effect does this have on the operation of the buzzer?

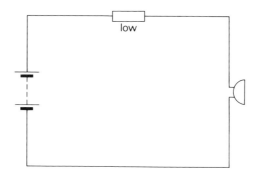

Project   A very simple burglar alarm

The problem is to use an LDR module, a buzzer module and a battery to construct a circuit which will sound an alarm when a light is switched on. If a burglar were foolish enough to turn on the light in a room he had entered, or if the light from his torch fell on the LDR, the circuit could be used to warn the householder.

21

Resistance

All you need to know about resistors in this course is that they can have different resistances. Resistance is measured by scientists in units called *ohms*. The values of the resistances in the resistor module are about 27 thousand ohms ('high'), about 2.7 thousand ohms ('medium') and about 270 ohms ('low'). The resistance of the LDR is perhaps a million ohms in the dark, falling to about 100 ohms in a bright light.

The motor

The symbol used in this book for the motor in a circuit diagram is this:

Experiment 3.6   The motor module
1. Connect the motor module to the battery. What happens when the current flows?

2. Reverse the battery connections to the motor. What difference does it make?

The above experiment shows that the motor can be driven in either direction depending on the direction in which the current flows through it. It is not always easy to see which

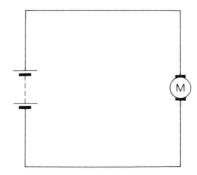

way the motor in the module is rotating. You could add a small propeller made from thin card to help. An interesting extension to this experiment would be to add a green and a red LED to the circuit in such a way that the red LED lights when the motor rotates one way and the green LED lights when it rotates the other.

Background reading

Microelectronics and the motor car
Microelectronics is about to play a large part in the motor car. It is now possible to buy cars with computer-controlled carburation, which is extremely efficient. It will not be long before it will be in all family cars.

Speedometers which compute your average speed and fuel gauges which 'tell' you in synthetic speech when your petrol is low will be around shortly, and so will headlights which come on automatically when the daylight falls below a certain level.

Another useful electronic device will be a microprocessor which computes the speed of the car travelling in front and assesses whether the two vehicles are being driven at a safe distance apart.

This kind of thing will, presumably, encourage more careful driving, once motorists have got used to the idea of being ticked off by their own cars. But vehicles which pepper one with spoken warnings and instructions may never be popular – a horrific new breed of back-seat drivers.

(Based on *The Mighty Micro* by Christopher Evans, published by Victor Gollancz.)

Chapter 4 **Switches**

In this book we shall consider a number of different types of electrical switch. Switching plays a very large and important part in modern electronics. Computers, for example, use electronic switches of various kinds, and the fact that computers can be used to control robots or aeroplanes is a result of their ability to switch things on and off.

The simplest switch is an on/off switch. The symbol for such a switch in a circuit diagram is shown below on the left. We know that a current will not flow in a circuit which has a gap in it: when the switch is open, there is a gap, but when it is closed the circuit is completed and a current flows.

The push-button switch is a type of on/off switch that makes contact when the button is pressed. The symbol used for it in this book is shown on the right.

Experiment 4.1 Circuits with switches

1. Connect a battery, an LED module and a push-button switch in series so that you can switch the LED on or off.

2. Now connect the battery, two LED modules in parallel and one switch so that you can switch both LEDs on or off at the same time.

3. Finally, connect the battery, two LED modules and two switches so that one switch operates one of the LEDs and the other switch operates the other LED.

4. When you have arranged your apparatus to work as described in **3**, draw a circuit diagram of it.

Questions for homework or class discussion

1. Describe what will happen to each of the lamps in the circuits below when the switches are closed (they are drawn in the open position).

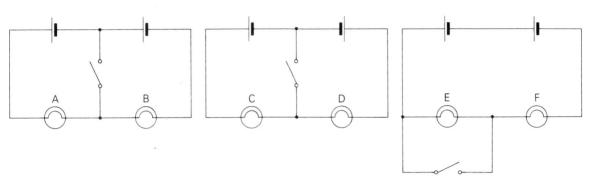

2. The circuit on the left shows one cell, two similar lamps (X and Y) and two switches A and B (shown in the open position). When the cell is connected across one lamp it glows with *normal brightness*. Copy the following table and state whether, on each occasion, each lamp will be bright, dim or out.

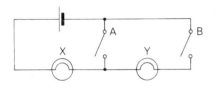

Switch positions	Lamp X	Lamp Y
A open, B open A open, B closed A closed, B open A closed, B closed		

3. Describe the effect of opening and closing the switches in each of the following circuits.

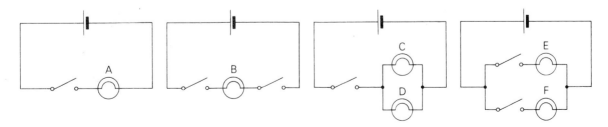

25

Experiment 4.2   The push-button switch

This experiment is the same as Experiment 4.1, part 3. If you did not succeed earlier, try it again. Use a battery, two push-button switches and red and green LED modules.

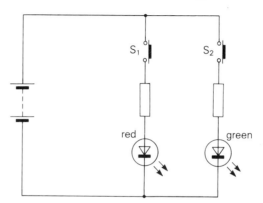

1. What happens when S_1 is pressed? What happens when it is released?

2. What happens when S_2 is pressed?

3. What happens when both are pressed?

The pressure pad as a switch

The pressure pad illustrated in the photograph is another form of on/off switch, in which the contacts are normally open. In other words, the two leads coming from it are not connected. As soon as any pressure is applied to the pad (by stepping or sitting on it), the switch is closed and the two leads are connected.

Projects with a pressure pad

1. Arrange a pressure pad, buzzer and battery so that the buzzer sounds whenever someone sits on a chair (it would be best to hide the pressure pad under a cushion).

2. Arrange a pressure pad under a mat outside the door of a classroom so that a warning is given when the teacher is approaching.

Experiment 4.3   Simple AND circuit

1. Connect two push-button switch modules in series with an LED module and a battery as shown below.

2. What happens when S_1 alone is pressed?

3. What happens when S_2 alone is pressed?

4. What happens when both switches are pressed at the same time?

5. Why do you think this is called an AND circuit?

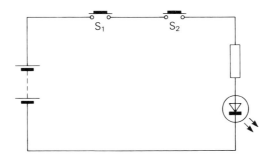

Experiment 4.4   Simple OR circuit

1. Using the same modules as in the last experiment, set up the circuit shown below.

2. What happens when S_1 alone is pressed?

3. What happens when S_2 alone is pressed?

4. Why do you think this is called an OR circuit?

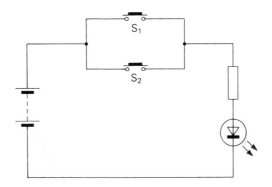

Uses of AND and OR circuits

There are many situations in which an AND circuit might be useful. For example, in a motor car we might want a 'ready to start' light to come on only when the driver has fixed his seat-belt AND closed his door. In a bank, it would be a useful precaution if the door to the strong room could be opened only when a switch beside the door AND a switch on the manager's desk were pressed at the same time. Can you think of any more?

An obvious use for an OR circuit is a simple burglar alarm. A pressure pad is placed under a carpet near a door so that the switch is closed by the pressure of the intruder's foot. The OR circuit could be used to protect two doors. An alarm would sound if entry were through either door 1 OR door 2. Can you think of any more uses of an OR circuit?

The double throw switch

A simple on/off switch, whose symbol is shown below, is

sometimes called an SPST switch, which stands for a 'Single Pole Single Throw' switch. There is one moving contact (the pole) and there is one position where it makes contact (the throw).

Included with your electronics apparatus there are SPDT switch modules. This switch is a 'Single Pole Double Throw'

S.P.D.T. SWITCH

switch and the symbol for it is shown above. When the switch is in one position, the lead A is connected to B; when it is in its other position, lead A is connected to C. It is sometimes called a *change-over* switch.

Another type of switch (though not included with your apparatus) is a DPDT switch. This is a 'Double Pole Double Throw' switch and it is like two SPDT switches linked so that they switch over together, as shown on the left.

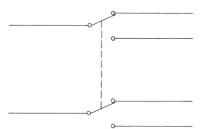

Project   Manual control of 'stop–go' traffic lights

A *single* set of 'stop–go' traffic lights is to be used to control cars entering a car park through a single lane. The operator sits at one end of the lane to control the lights so that, when a car is leaving, other cars are stopped from entering.

The operator could use the circuit of Experiment 4.2 on page 26 to control the lights, but this would not be very satisfactory. Why not?

Instead, use a red and a green LED module together with an SPDT switch and a battery to show how a more satisfactory system could be constructed.

In practice, it would be better if he had *two* sets of lights, each having a green and a red lamp. Devise a circuit which will allow cars to pass through the lane safely from either end. You will need two red LED modules, two green LED modules, an SPDT switch and a battery.

Project   Staircase lighting

The problem is to use two SPDT switch modules together with an LED module and a battery to construct a simple staircase lighting system. Suppose one switch is at the top of the stairs and the other at the bottom. It must be possible to turn the light on or off using *either* switch.

Experiment 4.5   Experiment with a motor

The circuit below involves two SPDT switch modules, a battery and the motor module. This is a problem experiment in that you should look carefully at the circuit diagram to decide for yourself what it will do. When you have decided, set up the apparatus to find out if you were correct.

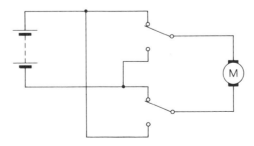

The reed switch

The symbol used in this book for a reed switch is shown below.

Experiment 4.6   Reed switch and magnet

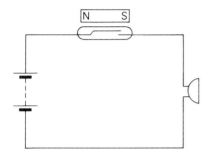

1. Take the reed switch module and examine the two metal contacts inside the glass envelope with a magnifying glass. These contacts are normally open. Bring a magnet to the side of the glass envelope as shown on the left and listen as you do so to see if you can hear a click as the contacts come together.

2. Then connect the switch in series with a buzzer and a battery.

3. Bring a small bar magnet close to the reed switch. What happens? What must have happened inside the glass envelope? Use your magnifying glass to see if you are right.

The reed switch consists of two metal contacts (called 'reeds') inside a glass envelope filled with an inactive (inert) gas to prevent corrosion. Since the reeds are made of a metal containing iron, they can be magnetised by a magnet. If the magnet is brought close to the switch as shown on the left, the metal strips are magnetised, one end being a north pole and the other a south. They are therefore attracted to each other, so that contact is made.

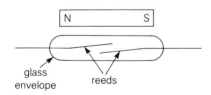

glass
envelope   reeds

As the magnet is taken away, the strength of the magnetism in the reeds decreases and the springiness of the metal is able to pull the contacts apart again.

In the reed switch module, there is either a resistor or a fuse in series with the switch to make sure that the current is never too big to damage the switch. In the circuit diagrams in this book we will not draw this safety device.

The above switch is an SPST switch: it is either open or closed. We shall later make use of a reed switch which

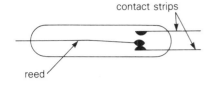

contact strips

reed

behaves as an SPDT switch. In this switch there is one long reed which acts as the pole of the switch, and two short contact strips. The reed is at first in contact with the lower contact strip, which is made from a non-magnetic material. But when the magnet is brought near, the reed and the top contact strip are magnetised and they come together.

The reed relay

When you first learnt about electric current, you found that it had both a heating and a magnetic effect. If a current is passed through a small coil, the coil behaves like a magnet.

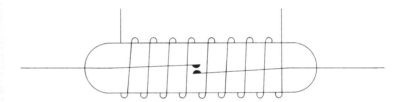

The reed relay consists of a reed switch like the one you have used, but it is not operated by a magnet. Instead, it has a coil around it as shown. If a current passes, the coil behaves like a magnet and, if the current is large enough, the reed switch closes.

In circuit diagrams it would be confusing to draw the coil round the reed switch, so it is usual to draw it at one side, as shown below.

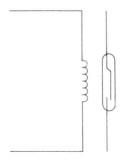

Experiment 4.7   The reed relay

1. Using the reed relay module, a push-button switch, an LED module and two batteries, set up the circuit below.

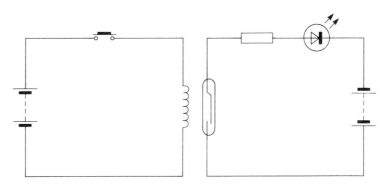

2. What happens to the LED when the push-button switch is closed?

This is an important experiment because this time the switching is produced by the flow of an electric current. The two circuits in the experiment are quite separate from each other, but what happens in one is controlled by what happens in the other.

In practice the current through the coil, which is needed to operate the reed switch, is usually much smaller than the current through the switch contacts. If the LED and resistor were replaced by an electric motor needing a much larger current to make it work, it could be controlled by a much smaller current passing through the coil circuit.

A good example of this is the starter motor of a car. The starter motor may require a very large current of about 50 amperes. This means that the leads from the battery to the motor need to be as short as possible, and, in any case, you do not want large currents of that size going to the dash-board of the car. So a much smaller current is switched on at the dash-board by the ignition switch, and this operates a relay which switches on the much larger current for the starter motor.

Using one circuit to control another plays an important part in electronics. The next experiment is another illustration of this.

Experiment 4.8 The reed relay used to control a motor

1. Use the LDR module, the reed relay module, the motor module and two batteries to set up the circuit below.

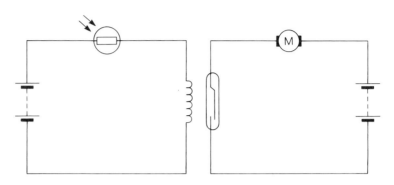

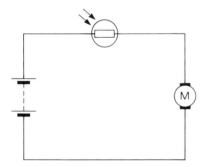

2. What happens to the motor when the LDR is covered up? What happens when a light is shone on the LDR?

3. If possible, put an ammeter in each circuit. Is the current in the first circuit very much less than that in the second?

4. You may wonder why it is necessary to use the reed relay at all in the above experiment. Why not use the circuit on the left where the LDR operates the motor directly? Try it and see.

It does not work because the motor needs a large current to operate it and the resistance of the LDR does not decrease enough to make it possible. Even if the resistance of the LDR did fall to a low enough value, it would probably be damaged by the very large current needed to operate the motor.

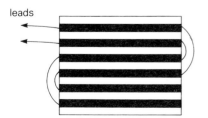

leads

Project   An automatically controlled washing line

A rain sensor can be made with two strips of metal which do not touch each other – as shown on the left. No electrical contact is made between the strips until some rain water falls and 'bridges' one of the gaps.

The problem is to use two batteries, the reed relay module,

the electric motor module and the rain sensor to make a circuit which switches on an electric motor when the rain falls. Such a circuit could be used for an automatically controlled washing line to bring in the washing when the rain starts to fall!

The experiment will not work with ordinary tap water because your relay is not sufficiently sensitive. However adding a pinch of salt makes the water an excellent conductor and the necessary complete circuit is provided. (If a real automatically controlled washing line were to be made, a more complicated circuit would be needed to make it sensitive enough to operate the relay when the rain began to fall.)

Experiment 4.9 Controlling a motor with a single power supply

1. In Experiment 4.8, two batteries were used. In this experiment, only one battery will be used. Set up the circuit below with one battery, a reed relay module, a push-button switch and the motor module.

2. What happens to the motor when the switch is closed?

3. In this circuit the relay coil and the relay contacts are connected in parallel. Copy the diagram and mark it with arrows to show the direction of the currents from the battery through each branch of the circuit and back to the battery again.

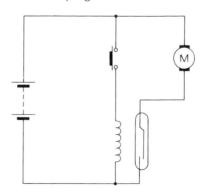

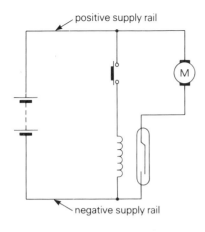

positive supply rail

M

negative supply rail

On page 19, we mentioned that it was useful to think of positive and negative supply rails. The top horizontal line in the circuit is the positive supply rail; the bottom horizontal line is the negative supply rail. In each of the parts of the circuit the current flows from the positive to the negative supply rail.

Try replacing the push-button switch by an LDR to make a light-controlled motor. As in Experiment 4.8, the current through the coil is much smaller than the current through the motor. The smaller current through the coil branch of the parallel circuit is now controlling the much bigger current through the motor branch.

Background reading

Locks in the future

A familiar old gadget which has been around for hundreds of years is just about to be pensioned off for ever – the key. Already you can obtain electronic locks which open when you punch in the appropriate combination, though they do rely on your remembering what the combination is. Human memory being as fallible as it is, the next development must be a lock which opens only when it has had the chance to scan the electronic chip built into a watch or a signet ring. No one will ever need to hide a key under the mat again. (From *The Mighty Micro* by Christopher Evans, published by Victor Gollancz.)

The photograph shows an automatic device by which a bank dispenses money after you present a credit card and type in your code. This is similar to the above.

You could use your electronic modules to design a safety device for a bank vault safe. Suppose a motor is needed to open the door of the vault with one switch outside the door and the other in the manager's office. The motor only works when both switches are pressed at the same time.

1. Describe the effect of closing the switch in each of the following circuits.

In which circuit will the cell(s) run down most quickly when the switch is closed?

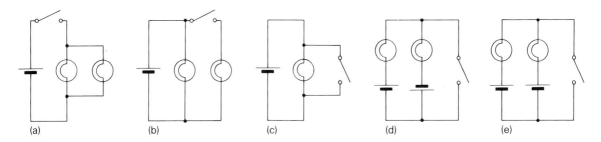

(a)   (b)   (c)   (d)   (e)

2. Here are three circuits containing a cell, an ammeter, a lamp, a resistor and a switch.

a. In which circuit does the ammeter measure the current passing through the lamp whether the switch is open or closed?

b. In which circuit does the ammeter measure the current through the lamp only when the switch is open?

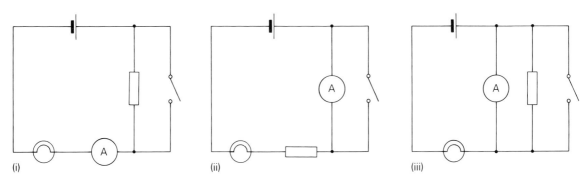

(i)   (ii)   (iii)

3. What do the following symbols stand for?

(a) (b) (c) (d) (e)

4. Draw the circuit symbol used for each of the following:
a. an LDR,
b. a motor,
c. a push-button switch,
d. a variable resistor,
e. a buzzer.

5. For each of the following, say what the letters stand for and why the component is so called:
a. an LED,
b. an LDR,
c. an SPST switch,
d. an SPDT switch.

6. This is a portrait of Sir Kit Cymbols. How many can you find and what do they represent?

7. In the circuit below, the resistance of the variable resistor, R, is to be reduced from its largest value to a very low value. Describe what you would see happening.

What additional component would you put in the circuit so that R could be varied over its full range safely?

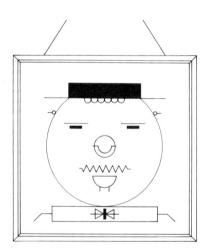

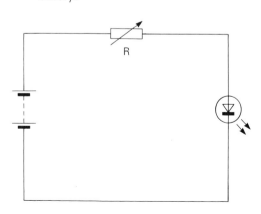

8. There are 10 errors in the circuit diagram below. Draw the diagram with the errors corrected.

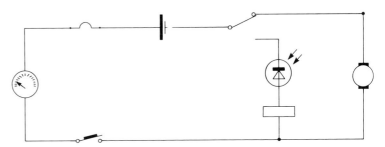

9. A reed switch works better if the magnet is held in the position shown in diagram (a) than it does in the position shown in diagram (b). Explain why.

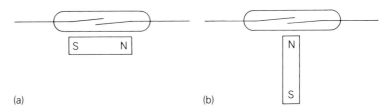

(a)   (b)

10. The circuit shown has two SPDT switches, A and B, in it.

a. The table shows the four possible arrangements for switches A and B, but the column showing whether the lamp is on or off has not been completed. Copy the table and complete it.

b. Where are you likely to find a circuit similar to this one being used?

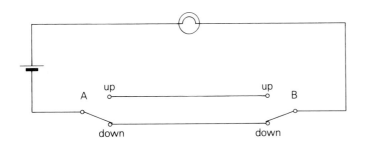

Position of A	Position of B	Lamp
down	down	
down	up	
up	down	
up	up	

11. The table on the right shows the four possible arrangements for the SPDT switches, A and B, in the circuit. Copy the table and complete it to show whether each of the lamps, X, Y and Z is on or off.

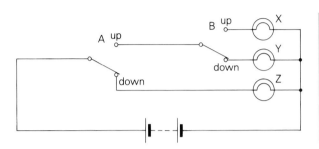

Position of A	Position of B	X	Y	Z
down	down			
down	up			
up	down			
up	up			

12. Complete a table (like the one in question 10) for the circuit below, which contains three switches. Note that there are eight possible arrangements with three switches. How many arrangements would be possible if a circuit had four SPDT switches in it?

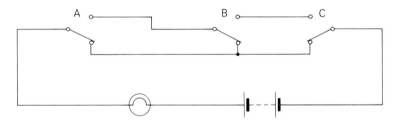

13. A room has three doors in it. Near each door, there is a switch which can switch the light in the room on or off, no matter how the other switches are set. The switches needed are shown, but the circuit has not been completed. Copy the diagram and complete the circuit.

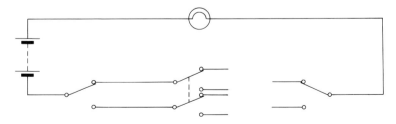

14. Here are two circuits, (a) and (b). What happens, in each circuit, when the switches are operated?
Why is (a) a much better circuit to use than (b)?

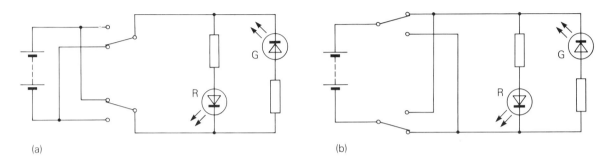

(a)   (b)

15. Two SPST reed switches can be used to make a DPST switch.
  a. What do SPST and DPST stand for?
  b. How does a DPST switch differ from two push-button switches?
  c. How can two reed switches be made into a DPST switch if only one coil is available?
  d. How can a DPST arrangement be made by using two SPST *relays*, that is, two SPST reed switches each with its own coil? Draw a circuit diagram.

16. What is it that is measured in (i) amperes, (ii) ohms?
  a. How many millimetres are there in 1 metre?
  b. How many milliamperes (mA) are there in 1 ampere (1 A)?
  c. How many metres are there in 1 kilometre?
  d. How many ohms are there in 1 kilohm?

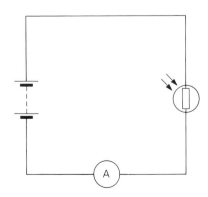

17. In the circuit on the left, the light falling on the LDR causes it to have a resistance of 100 ohms, and the ammeter reads 60 mA (60 milliamps). The light falling on the LDR changes and the ammeter then reads 6 mA.
  a. Did the resistance of the LDR become greater or smaller?
  b. Did the light get more or less bright?
  c. What do you think the new resistance of the LDR was?

18. In the circuit shown, the ammeter reads 10 mA.
  a. What is the colour of the terminal X of the ammeter?
  b. When switch S is closed, the ammeter reading becomes 30 mA. What is the current at each of the points A, B, C, D, E and F?

  The battery and ammeter are now reversed and the meter reads 28 mA with S closed.
  c. Why does the ammeter have to be reversed when the battery is reversed?
  d. What is now the current at each of the points A, B, C, D, E and F?
  e. Finally, the non-conducting diode is reversed. What does the ammeter now read?

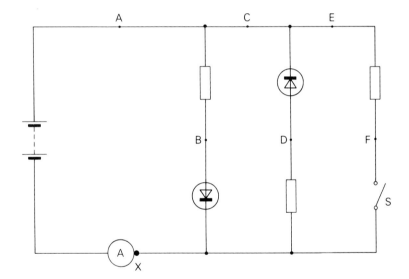

19. Draw a circuit diagram of a circuit which will allow you to reverse the direction of rotation of a motor with the aid of two SPDT switches. Include in your circuit a green LED and a red LED so that the LED lit changes when the direction of rotation of the motor changes.

20. When is it of advantage to use a relay in a circuit? Give some examples of possible uses.

21. (For fun!) A pupil tries to set up a circuit but he jumbles the wires together. To which of A, B, C, D or E should the lead from the battery be joined in order to

a. sound the buzzer,

b. light the lamp,

c. work the motor?

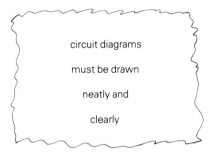

circuit diagrams

must be drawn

neatly and

clearly

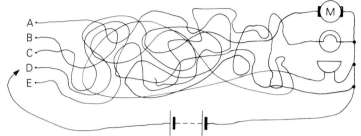

A connection to one of the wires might be dangerous. Which one? Why might it be dangerous?

22. In most cars, the interior light comes on when either of the two front doors is opened. Each door operates an SPST switch which is in the open position when the door is closed.

a. Is an OR circuit or an AND circuit needed to do this? Explain your answer.

b. Draw a diagram of a circuit which would work in this way.

c. Add to your diagram another switch which would allow the driver to switch the light on if both doors were closed.

23. A spin drier has a start–stop switch, but the motor will only spin the drum if the lid is closed. Closing the lid closes an SPST switch inside the machine, and the motor can then be started with the start–stop switch.

a. Is an OR circuit or an AND circuit needed? Explain your answer.

b. Draw a diagram of a simple circuit which could be used.

c. Add a buzzer to your circuit diagram so that the buzzer will sound if the lid is not closed and the start-stop switch is operated. (Remember that a buzzer requires much less current than a motor does.)

Chapter 6 **Electrical pressure**

Suppose you have two syringes, A and B, with a tube fixed between them, and that the space inside is full of water.

A   B

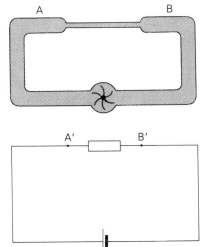

You can make water pass from A to B through the tube by pressing the piston of syringe A. Doing this makes the pressure in A greater than the pressure in B and this *difference* in pressure causes water to flow through the tube. The harder you push on the piston of A, the greater is the pressure difference and the faster the water flows so that there is a bigger current. Of course, the current will stop when you stop pushing or when the piston cannot move any further.

If a current is to flow all the time, then a water pump has to be used to maintain a difference in pressure between A and B.

This is just like an electrical circuit in which there is a cell (an electricity 'pump') causing electric current to flow through a resistance wire. The cell pumps electric charge through the wire, and we call that movement of charge an electric current. The cell causes a difference of electrical 'pressure' between A' and B', and the effect of this is an electric current flowing from A' to B' through the resistance wire.

If the pipe between A and B in the water circuit is shorter, then the same difference of pressure between A and B causes a larger current, because it is easier to push water through a short pipe than through a long one. And the electrical circuit is like that, too – a shorter piece of resistance wire allows a larger current to flow. What do you think would be the effect of using a fatter wire?

There are other similarities between water circuits and electrical circuits.

1. If the circuits have parallel branches, some current flows through each branch. For both circuits, the sum of the currents flowing in each branch equals the current flowing from the pump.

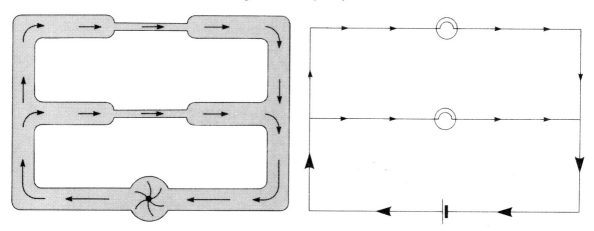

2. If one of the pipes had a stop-tap in it, we could use the tap to stop the water current even with the pump still working. The water pressure on one side of the tap would then be bigger than on the other side, but water could not pass through the tap.

   Electrical circuits can be like that if we put a switch in the circuit: there is no current when there is a gap in the circuit, but there is a pressure difference across the switch.

3. Notice, too, that the water pump does not create water! The water is there all the time, and all the pump does is to move it through the pipes. So it is with the electrical circuit. The battery does not manufacture electric charge. The electric charge is in the wires all the time, and all the cell does is to move the charge through the wires.

Measuring electrical pressure difference

In a water circuit we could measure the difference in pressure between the two sides of the pump by inserting a long tube on each side of it. On one side of the pump, the pressure would be 'high' and on the other side 'low', and the difference in pressure would be measured by the difference in the levels of the water in the two tubes.

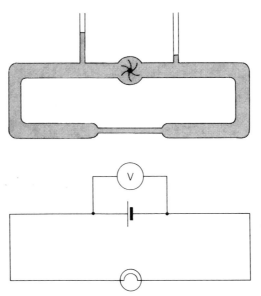

Electrical pressure difference is measured with an instrument called a 'voltmeter' (and in a unit called a volt). The circuit diagram symbol for it is shown below. As with the

water circuit, the voltmeter has to be connected between the points whose pressure difference we require; that is to say, it is connected in parallel with the cell or *across* it. Notice that this is different from the ammeter which is connected in a circuit in series.

Like an ammeter, the voltmeter must be connected the right way round. One terminal is usually coloured red (or marked +) and this should be connected to the positive side of the cell, or the point where the pressure is higher. The other terminal is usually black (or marked −), and this should be connected to the negative side of the cell, or the point where the pressure is lower.

Experiment 6.1   Using a voltmeter

1. Connect three cells in series as shown. Measure the pressure difference or voltage between P and Q with a voltmeter. Note its reading.

2. Now measure the voltage between Q and R, and then between R and S. The readings should all be close to 1.5 volts.

3. Then measure the voltage of two cells (between P and R, or between Q and S). Finally, measure the voltage of three cells in series (between P and S).

Each of the cells you have used produces a pressure difference of about 1.5 volts, or 1.5 V. A battery of two cells in series produces twice as much, about 3.0 V, and a battery of three cells gives 4.5 V. Batteries using this type of cell and giving 3, 4.5, 6 or 9 V can be bought. Different kinds of cell can be obtained; one type produces 1.2 V, another 2.0 V, for example. See if you can find out what voltage a car battery gives, and how many cells there are in it.

Putting cells in series to form a battery produces a more powerful 'pump', and more powerful pumps cause more current to pass through a circuit. The voltage from a cell or battery remains fairly steady over most of its life and then falls towards the end of it. A graph of its voltage against time might look like this, though how rapidly it falls depends on the current which flows through it.

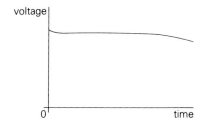

Cells in parallel

Until now, we have considered only cells in series. The next experiment deals with cells in parallel.

Experiment 6.2   Cells in parallel

1. Connect a voltmeter across one cell and measure the electrical pressure difference it causes.

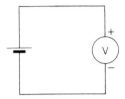

2. Add another cell in parallel with the first, taking care to make sure the cells have their positive terminals connected together. What is the voltage now?

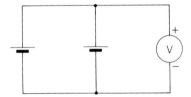

3. Try adding a third cell. Does this change the voltage?

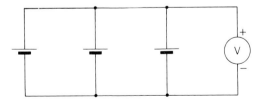

Connecting cells in parallel does not change the voltage produced. A lamp connected across the cell arrangements shown above would light with normal brightness in each case. So, what would be the difference?

4. Connect the circuit shown below, and use an ammeter to measure the current flowing.

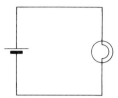

5. Now add a second cell in parallel, as shown, and measure the current at each of the points, X, Y and Z. What do you notice?

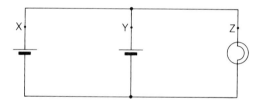

You should find that the current through the lamp in each circuit is about the same, but the current through each cell in 5 is only half the value it was in 4. Can you guess the current which would flow through each cell if a third cell in parallel were added?

The advantage of having cells in parallel is that they last longer when each has to push a smaller current.

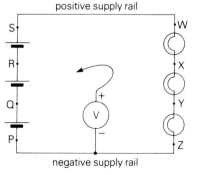

positive supply rail

negative supply rail

Voltage levels

Experiment 6.3   Measuring voltage levels
1. Set up the circuit shown, with the black (−) terminal of the voltmeter connected to the negative supply rail.

2. Connect the red (+) terminal of the voltmeter to P, and note the reading.

3. Connect the red (+) terminal, in turn, to Q, R, S, W, X, Y and Z, and note the readings.

In this experiment, you are measuring the electrical pressure difference between a certain point in the circuit and the negative supply rail where the pressure is lowest. You are measuring how high the level at that point is above the lowest level. The level at Q is about 1.5 V, at R about 3 V, at S about 4.5 V. The level drops in similar steps from W to X to Y to Z. At the points P and Z the level is the same as that of the black terminal of the voltmeter, and so the voltmeter gives a zero reading.

In the final chapters of this book, we shall often use the idea of voltage levels (with respect to the negative power rail). We shall refer to the level of the positive supply rail as the HIGH level and that of the negative supply rail as the LOW level.

Of course, if a conductor of any sort is connected between different levels, the electrical pressure difference will cause a current to flow through the conductor. But, if the ends of a conductor are connected to the same voltage level, then no current will flow through it because there is no electrical pressure difference to cause it.

Chapter 7 **A special relay circuit**

Radios and television sets, record players and tape recorders, digital watches and computers, contain circuits designed by electronics engineers to be useful to us.

In designing these circuits, the engineers frequently use a number of smaller, simpler circuits which are connected together in a suitable way to do what is required. They know how to do this because they are familiar with the ways in which the simpler circuits behave. In other words, they use these simpler circuits as 'building bricks' when constructing more complicated circuits.

In this chapter you will find out about one of the most important electronic building bricks and you will use it to do some useful jobs. It is a circuit with a reed relay in it, but there is no need at this stage to understand how the circuit works. If you would like to know, you will find an explanation in the next chapter. It is usually referred to as a NAND circuit, but even that name need not worry you at this stage: we will discover later why it is called that.

The NAND relay module

In order that the NAND module shall work, it is necessary to connect it to a battery as shown. The positive terminal of the battery provides the positive supply rail, the negative

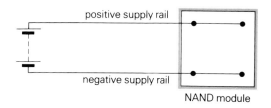

NAND module

terminal the negative supply rail. As explained in the previous chapter, there is a difference in voltage level between these two rails, and we shall refer to the level of the positive supply rail as the HIGH level and that of the negative supply rail as the LOW level.

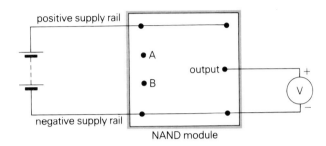

NAND module

The NAND module has two input sockets (labelled A and B in the above drawing) and an output socket. The voltage level at the output socket depends on the voltage levels at the A and B input sockets. To show the voltage level at the output socket, a voltmeter can be connected between it and the negative supply rail as shown in the diagram above.

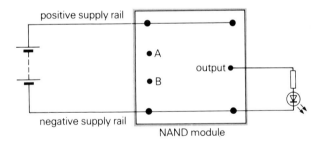

NAND module

Another way to show the voltage level at the output is to connect an LED module between the output socket and the negative supply rail, as shown in the drawing above. Then, if the voltage at the output is HIGH (that is, at the level of the positive supply rail), a current will flow through the LED to the negative supply rail. If the voltage at the output socket is LOW (that is, at the level of the negative supply rail), no current will flow and the LED will not light. (Of course, this assumes that the LED has been connected the right way round; if it were the wrong way round, it would not light!)

Experiment 7.1 Using the NAND relay module as an INVERTER

1. Set up the circuit below using a NAND relay module, an LED module and a battery.

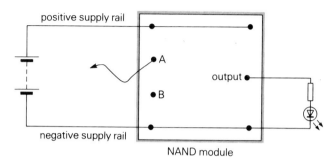

positive supply rail

A

output

B

negative supply rail

NAND module

2. Plug a lead into input socket A. Such a lead, the other end of which is not connected at first to anything, is often called a 'flying lead'. Connect the other end of the lead to the positive supply rail. What does the LED tell you?

3. Now connect the flying lead (still connected to socket A) to the negative supply rail. What does the LED tell you this time?

4. Remove that lead and try the same experiment with the flying lead connected to input socket B. Is the behaviour the same as for input socket A?

5. When the flying lead is not connected to either of the supply rails, does the input behave as if it is HIGH or as if it is LOW?

You should have noticed that the output is at a HIGH level (LED alight) only when the input level is LOW, and that both inputs behave in the same way. When unconnected, an input behaves as though it is at the HIGH level. An unconnected input is usually said to be 'floating'.

This behaviour can be shown in what is called a truth table, as shown on the left.

Notice that the circuit changes the voltage level over; if you connect the input to the LOW level (the negative supply rail), the output goes to the HIGH level, and vice versa. It is

Input	Output
low	high
high	low

for this reason that the circuit is called an INVERTER ('invert' means 'turn upside down').

The circuit can be operated with a switch or an LDR at the input, and the output can be used to operate a buzzer or motor, as in the next experiment.

Experiment 7.2   Operating an INVERTER with an LDR

1. Use a NAND module, a buzzer module, an LDR module and a battery to set up the circuit:

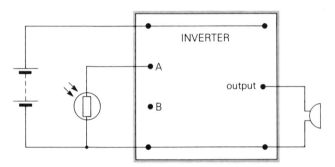

2. What happens when you shine the light from a torch on to the LDR?

When light is shone on the LDR its resistance becomes small and it behaves like a *closed* switch. This means that the input is effectively connected to the negative supply rail. It is therefore LOW and that means the output goes HIGH so that the buzzer sounds.

In the dark the resistance of the LDR is very high and it behaves like an *open* switch. The input is then unconnected (it is 'floating'), and you found in the last experiment that a floating input behaves as though it were HIGH. A HIGH input results in a LOW output, so the buzzer will be off.

Project   An automatic light

Use two NAND relay modules, an LDR module, an LED module and a battery to make a circuit which will light the LED automatically when it gets dark.

Experiment 7.3 Using both the inputs of the NAND module

1. Use a NAND module, an LED module and a battery to set up the circuit:

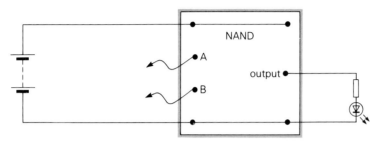

Input B	Input A	Output
low	low	
low	high	
high	low	
high	high	

2. Plug a flying lead into each of the inputs of the NAND module.

3. Make a copy of the truth table shown above. Connect each of the input leads to either the positive or negative supply rails in order to complete the truth table, showing whether the output is high or low. Remember that each of the input leads must be connected to either the positive supply rail or the negative supply rail.

Truth table for the NAND module

The truth table for the NAND module is as shown.

Input B	Input A	Output
low	low	high
low	high	high
high	low	high
high	high	low

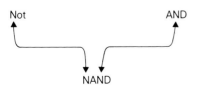

Notice that the output is HIGH whenever one or both inputs is at a LOW level. You could say that, with a NAND circuit, the output is:

Not high only when input A AND input B are high.

That is why it is called a NAND circuit.

An AND circuit

An AND circuit would have a different truth table. It would have a high output only if both inputs A AND B were high.

Input B	Input A	Output
low	low	low
low	high	low
high	low	low
high	high	high

Experiment 7.4 Making an AND circuit

1. Use two NAND relay modules (one as an INVERTER), an LED module and a battery to set up the circuit below.

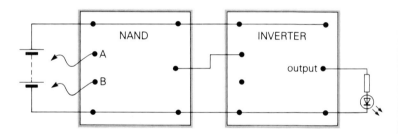

Input B	Input A	Output
low	low	
low	high	
high	low	
high	high	

2. Attach flying leads to each of the inputs A and B of the first NAND module. Copy the truth table. By connecting the flying leads to the positive or negative supply rails, complete the truth table. Does your circuit behave like an AND circuit?

3. Compare the truth table for this circuit with the table obtained for the NAND circuit. What has the INVERTER done?

Project A 'length' detector

Use an AND circuit, two LDR modules, a buzzer module and a battery so that, if both LDRs are darkened, the buzzer sounds. This circuit could be used to detect objects of length greater than the distance between the LDRs.

A convenient shorthand

It becomes a little tedious writing 'high' and 'low' in truth tables. Electronics engineers usually write '1' for 'high' and '0' for 'low'. Thus the truth table for a NAND circuit changes like this:

Input B	Input A	Output
low	low	high
low	high	high
high	low	high
high	high	low

becomes

Input B	Input A	Output
0	0	1
0	1	1
1	0	1
1	1	0

Practise the new shorthand by using it to rewrite the truth tables for the INVERTER and the AND circuit.

Experiment 7.5 Using a NAND circuit to make a simple burglar alarm

1. Use a NAND relay module, two push-button switches, a buzzer and a battery to connect the circuit:

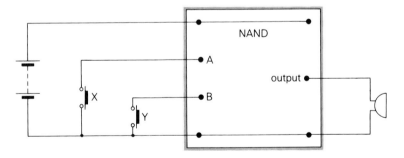

2. What happens when switch X or switch Y is pressed? What happens when both are pressed together? Explain why this happens.

3. It makes a more realistic burglar alarm if the push-button switches are replaced by pressure pads.

There is still a serious weakness in this simple circuit for use as a burglar alarm. The alarm stops when the intruder steps off the pressure pad. A better alarm would continue to sound once it had been set off, whether or not the switch was released. To make such an alarm, a circuit called a BISTABLE is needed. This can be made using two NAND modules and will be discussed in Chapter 9.

Background reading

Input – process – output
When you used a NAND module, you applied an input to it through its input terminals. Some process occurred inside the module. Then something happened at the output.

This is typical of modern electronics. It happens in computers: an input is processed into an output in a form convenient for use. This concept of input – process – output is not confined to electronics, as the following example shows.

Suppose you are running a dry-cleaning shop. The input consists of clothes delivered to the shop for cleaning. They go through the process of being cleaned, and then comes the output when they are packaged ready for the customer to collect. It is not necessary for the customers to understand the process: they are concerned only with the input and the output.

Of course a bit of organisation of the input may make the process more efficient – getting all the dresses together and all the suits – and the output can be organised in various ways.

The electronic modules you have used all have inputs and outputs, but the precise process inside does not really matter. Your NAND modules had reed relays in them, but other versions may have transistors inside them, or other forms of 'chip'.

Chapter 8 **How the NAND relay circuit works**

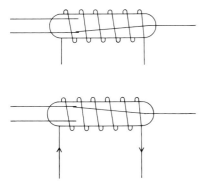

On page 31 we described the SPDT reed switch. The NAND relay module uses such a reed switch with a coil wound round it, as in the diagram.

The reed (the pole of the switch) is normally touching the lower of the two contacts, as shown. When a current flows through the coil, the coil magnetises the reed and the upper contact, so that the reed moves up to touch the upper contact. (The lower contact is made of a non-magnetic material so that it is not magnetised.) The reed stays in the upper position until the current in the coil stops flowing, when it springs back to touch the lower contact again.

How a reed relay works as an INVERTER
The battery provides the positive and negative supply rails – diagram (a).

An SPDT reed switch is connected between the positive rail and the negative rail as shown in (b). The pole of the switch is connected to the output point P, and this is normally touching the lower switch contact so that the output is low.

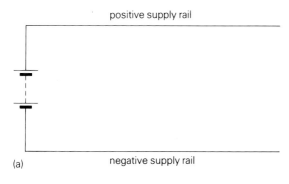

positive supply rail

negative supply rail

(a)

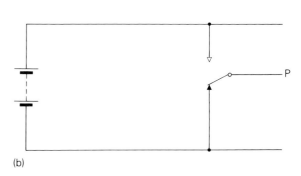

P

(b)

Round the reed switch is a coil, making it into a reed relay. In diagram (c) it would be confusing to draw the coil round the reed switch, so it has been drawn for convenience at the side. The coil is connected between the positive supply rail and the input A.

What happens if A is connected to the positive rail as in diagram (d)? As J and K are both at the same voltage level, no current will flow through the coil. The reed switch will not change. P will still be connected to the negative rail. Thus if A is HIGH, P is LOW.

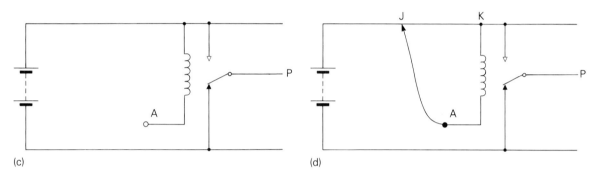

(c)

(d)

What happens if A is connected to the negative rail – diagram (e)? The coil is now connected between the positive and negative supply rails, so a current will flow through it from K to L. The current in the coil produces a magnetic field – and the reed switch changes over. P is now connected to the positive rail. Thus if A is LOW, P is HIGH.
The truth table is shown below. We have an INVERTER.

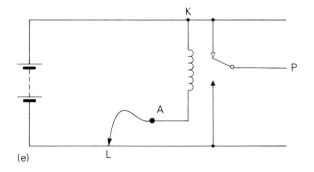

(e)

Input A	Output P		Input A	Output P
low high	high low	or	0 1	1 0

How a reed relay works as a NAND circuit

As on the previous page, the battery provides positive and negative supply rails and an SPDT reed switch is connected between them, with the pole connected to the output point P. Normally the pole is touching the lower switch contact so the output is LOW.

A coil is again round the reed switch, making it into a reed relay. But this time the coil is connected between the positive rail and *two* input points A and B, as shown in (b).

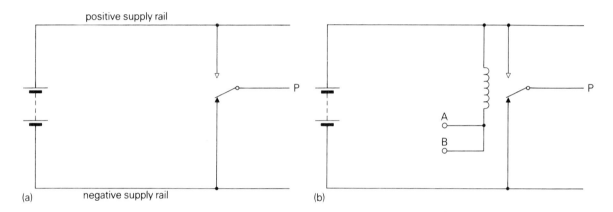

(a)

(b)

What happens if A and B are both connected to the positive rail (in other words, if A and B are both HIGH)? No current flows through the coil and the output therefore remains LOW.

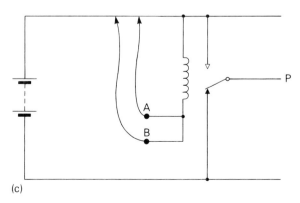

(c)

But if A and B are both connected LOW, a current flows through the coil, the reed switch changes and the output goes HIGH.

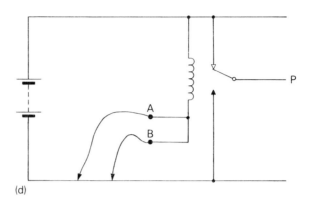

(d)

Input B	Input A	Output P
0	0	1
0	1	
1	0	
1	1	0

We have begun to complete a truth table, as shown on the left.

What happens if A is HIGH and B is LOW? A current would immediately flow, but not through the coil. Such connections would merely short circuit the supply and rapidly discharge the battery.

To prevent this happening, a diode is added near the input socket A as shown in diagram (e). Then as B is LOW, a current will now flow through the coil and the output goes HIGH.

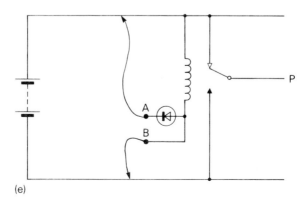

(e)

·What happens when B is HIGH and A is LOW? Again, the battery is short-circuited, and a second diode near B is needed. Now when B is HIGH and A is LOW, a current flows through the coil and the output is switched to HIGH.

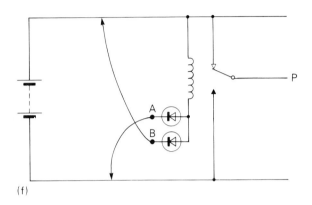

(f)

We can now complete the truth table:

Input B	Input A	Output P
0	0	1
0	1	1
1	0	1
1	1	0

and we have a NAND circuit.

The circuit is marked on the front of the NAND relay module. Remember, though, that you can use the NAND module to do useful jobs without understanding how it works. In electronics today even circuit design engineers use building bricks such as the NAND circuit without worrying about how they work. The important thing is to know what the building bricks do, and how to make use of them.

Background reading

Gates

In this book we have referred to the NAND 'module' or the NAND 'circuit'. The more usual term used by electronics engineers is 'gate'. They will refer to a NAND gate, an AND gate, an OR gate and so on. From the experiments in this book, it is not clear why this word 'gate' is used. It should be rather more obvious in later electronics work when you start to use pulses as the input to a module.

By a pulse we mean an input which is at a LOW level at one moment and then at a HIGH level and then at a LOW level again. A series of pulses is illustrated like this:

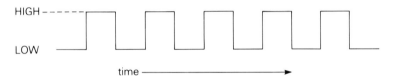

Such a series of pulses coming to a 'gate' may be applied to one of the inputs. If a similar series is then obtained at the output, the module would be behaving like a 'gate' – and in that case an *open* gate. On the other hand, if it does not appear at the output, the module would be like a *closed* gate.

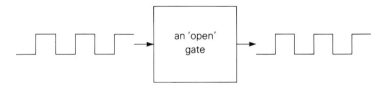

We shall not use the word 'gate' in this book, but we felt you would like to know about it as you may hear other people using the term.

Chapter 9 **The BISTABLE**

In this chapter you will connect two NAND modules together in a new way to make what is called a bistable circuit. Bistable circuits are used a great deal in modern electronics, especially in computers. After learning how to make a BISTABLE, and after you have found out what it does, you will have the chance to build some useful circuits with it.

Experiment 9.1   Making a bistable circuit

1. Set up the circuit below using two NAND modules, two LED modules and a battery. The two NAND modules have the same positive and negative supply rails.

    The LED modules are connected between the outputs of the NAND modules and the negative supply rail. They will show whether the outputs are HIGH or LOW.

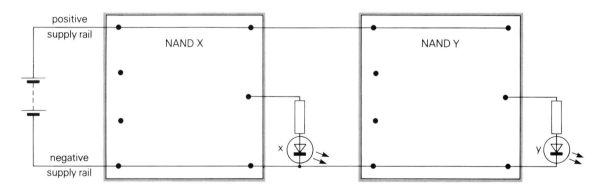

2. Now add a lead which connects the output of NAND X to one of the inputs of NAND Y. What do the LEDs show? (As there are no connections to the inputs of NAND X, the output of NAND X is LOW, and therefore the input of NAND Y must also be LOW. And that means that the output of NAND Y must therefore be HIGH and LED y is lit.)

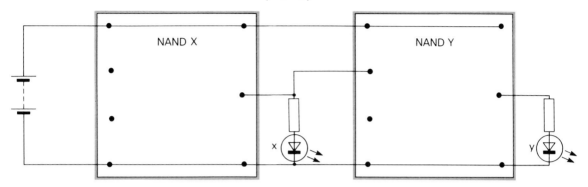

3. Next, connect a lead from the output of NAND Y to one of the inputs of NAND X. (Note that in drawing this in the diagram below, it is necessary for the lead from NAND Y to cross over the positive supply rail. This does *not* mean that they make electrical contact. If they were connected there would be a dot at the junction.)

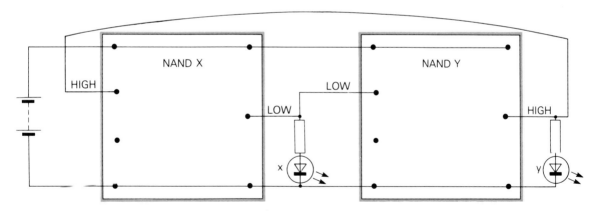

When NAND Y's output is connected to the input of NAND X, it makes that input HIGH. This does not change the output of NAND X, which remains LOW. LED x remains unlit.

However long the connections are left, LED x remains unlit and LED y remains lit. It is a *stable* arrangement.

4. But this is not the only stable arrangement. Remove the two leads connecting together the inputs and outputs of NAND X and NAND Y. Then connect first the output of NAND Y to the input of NAND X and afterwards connect the output of NAND X to the input of NAND Y. You will now have set up the other stable arrangement. How does this second stable state of affairs differ from the first one?

In the first state,   LED x is unlit,   LED y is lit.
In the second state,   LED x is lit,   LED y is unlit.

Because the circuit has two stable states, it is called a bistable circuit.

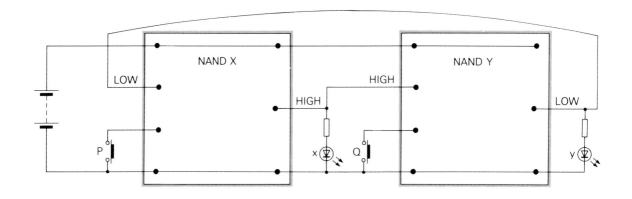

5. Now add two push-button switches to the arrangement of modules, as shown. What happens when you press switch Q? Try pressing it several times.

6. What happens when you press switch P? Try pressing it several times.

7. Now press Q again, and then P. Then press P and Q one after the other.

Pressing a switch causes the BISTABLE to switch from one of its stable states to the other, *provided* it is the switch connected to the NAND module whose output is LOW (that is, the one with the LED not lit).

In the first diagram below, it is only when you press Q that the circuit flips over to that shown in the second diagram. After it has flipped over, pressing Q again has no further effect.

When Q is pressed for the first time, the input of NAND Y is connected to the negative supply rail and the output of NAND Y becomes HIGH immediately. That gives a HIGH input to NAND X, so that its output becomes LOW. Because that is connected to the input of NAND Y, NAND Y now has a LOW input (and therefore a HIGH output) whether Q is pressed or not. The only way to get the BISTABLE to flop back again is to operate switch P. And now you can understand why bistable circuits are often called 'flip-flops'.

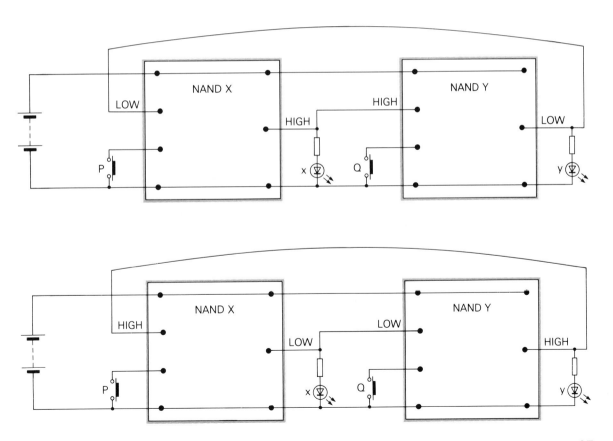

Experiment 9.2   A latched burglar alarm

Having built the BISTABLE, you are now in a position to build a really good burglar alarm.

1. First replace LED y with a buzzer. What happens when you switch from one stable state to the other?

2. Now replace the push-button switch Q at the input of the NAND Y module by a pressure pad. What happens when the pressure pad is pressed?

Project   Teacher warning system

A small variation of the arrangement in Experiment 9.2 will turn it into a 'teacher detector'. You could put a pressure pad under the mat in the corridor outside your classroom to let you know when your teacher is coming.

It would be better if the buzzer could be turned off before the teacher arrives. Perhaps this could be done by putting a second pressure pad under another mat immediately outside the door to change the BISTABLE back when the teacher steps on the mat.

The teacher will then automatically set off the alarm and silence it before entering the room. We leave that as something for you to try.

Project   Controlling an electric motor

Use two NAND relay modules (as a bistable circuit) and two push-button switches to control an electric motor so that, in one of the stable states, the motor goes one way round, and in the other state, it goes the opposite way.

Background reading

Controlling the speed of a motor

Lamps, motors and other devices can all be controlled by the output from a computer. Most microcomputers can provide an output voltage of 5 V, and the computer can be programmed so that this voltage is either on or off. In other words, assuming that 5 V is what we call HIGH and 0 V is what we call LOW, the computer can be programmed so that the output is switched to either HIGH or LOW. In turn this can be used to control a motor.

The computer can also be used to control the speed of the motor. This may seem surprising at first sight since the program merely switches the 5 V on or off and you might think that, to control the speed of the motor, you want to vary the voltage, and of course that cannot be done when all the computer can do is to switch on or off.

The control is achieved by switching the output HIGH for varying intervals of time. For example, in (a) below, the output is HIGH for more time than it is in case (b).

In case (a), more energy is transferred to the motor than in case (b), and so the motor rotates faster. It is in this way that the speed of the motor is controlled.

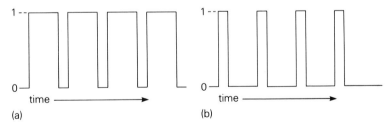

(a)   (b)

Chapter 10 **Problem solving**

At the end of Chapter 9, there was a project problem for you to solve. It was not a very hard one: you were told you had to make a motor turn round one way and then the other, and you saw how to do that in Experiment 3.6 on page 22. You know that if the motor is connected to the positive and negative supply rails as shown in diagram (a), it will turn round one way. If it is connected as in diagram (b), it will turn the other way.

positive or HIGH (M) negative or LOW
(a)

negative or LOW (M) positive or HIGH
(b)

Next, you were told that you had to make these voltage changes using the two stable states of a BISTABLE.

The two states are shown in diagrams (c) and (d). Can you see where the motor should be connected for the BISTABLE to control its direction of rotation?

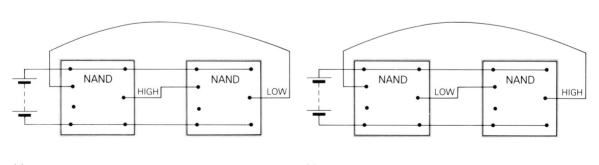

(c)   (d)

The last step of all is to connect into the circuit the two push-button switches which will be used to cause the BISTABLE to flip over from one stable state to the other. And you learnt how to do that in Experiment 9.1!

Now you can draw the circuit diagram of the circuit which solves the problem. Set it up and try it if you did not succeed before.

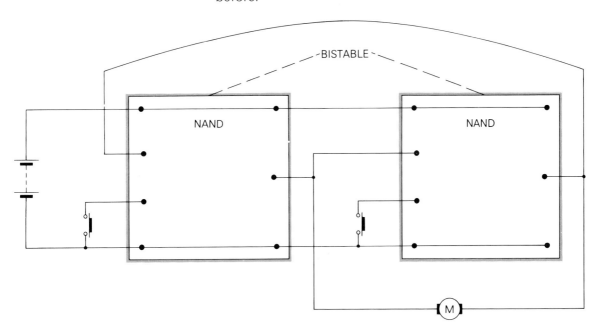

To solve that problem you had to know how to work the motor (the output component), which circuit to use to do it, and how to use the switches connected to the NAND modules (the input components) to make the circuit work as you wanted it to do. Then you drew a circuit diagram, set it up and tested it. All the project problems can be solved in this way, but you will not always be told which circuit you should use. Of course, if the circuit does not work correctly when you test it, then you have to think out why and put the error right.

On the next page there is another project problem for you to solve, but this time you are not told anything about the circuit you should use.

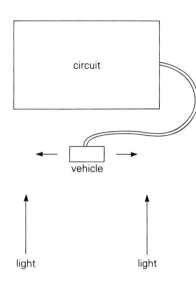

circuit

vehicle

light   light

Project   Vehicle moving backwards and forwards between light beams

A vehicle driven by an electric motor, such as a model car or train, is to move backwards and forwards between two beams of light.

Suppose the vehicle is moving to the left. When it interrupts the light beam on the left, the circuit must reverse the motor so that the vehicle moves to the right. And then, when it interrupts the right-hand light beam, the circuit must reverse the motor again.

It seems that this project is very similar to the previous one. There are two states for the vehicle: moving to the left and moving to the right. This suggests you should use a bistable circuit. And the bistable circuit needs to be switched from one stable state to the other by input components which are sensitive to light instead of push-button switches. That suggests that LDRs should be used.

So you might think the circuit shown below is the answer to the problem.

Would this circuit work? Think hard! What happens when the vehicle is between the light beams so that both LDRs are brightly illuminated?

If you still think it would work, set up the circuit and try it.

You will find that, when light falls on both LDRs, the motor does not work. This is because the resistance of an LDR is small when bright light falls on it. That means that

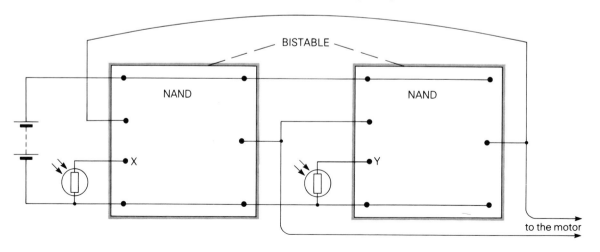

the inputs X and Y in the above circuit are connected to the negative supply rail. A current therefore flows through each of the relay coils in the NAND modules, and that means that both the outputs will be connected to the positive supply rail. Both the outputs are at the same HIGH level. With the wires of the motor joined to these outputs, no current will flow through the motor.

To get over this difficulty, what you now have to do is to find a way of making the inputs X and Y HIGH (instead of LOW) when light is falling on the LDRs. Can you think how to do that? Which extra circuit do you need? Look back to Experiment 7.2 on page 53.

If you use an INVERTER between each LDR and the input X or Y, then X and Y will be connected to the HIGH level when the LDR is brightly lit. And when both LDRs are illuminated, the BISTABLE will be in one of its stable states and the motor should turn.

The circuit diagram below has only been partly drawn. You should copy it and complete it.

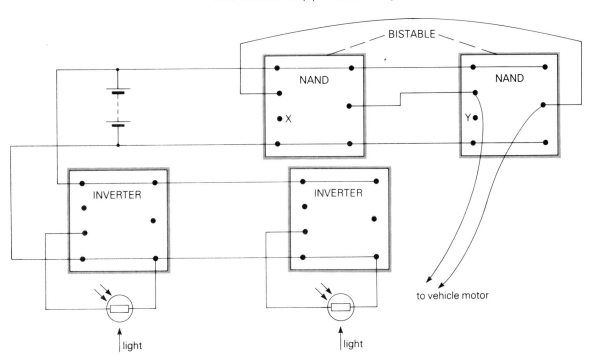

You may find that it still does not work as you expect, even though the LDRs are brightly lit and the vehicle moves. Perhaps the vehicle moves right through one of the beams without the BISTABLE switching to its other stable state. That could be because it has to be the *other* beam which needs to be interrupted to reverse the motor. How can that fault be put right? Try changing round the connections to the motor.

Solving other problems

Each project problem can be tackled in a similar way. First you must decide what is necessary to make the output components work, whether they are lamps, buzzers, motors or something else. Then you must decide which circuit to use to do that, and which input components are needed (switches, pressure pads, LDRs or something else).

Next draw a circuit diagram, check that it will work in the way you think it should, set it up and try it. If it does not do what you expect, try to work out why it is misbehaving. When you have done that, you should know how to put it right. The following are suggestions for further projects.

Project   Window alarm
Design a circuit which will sound an alarm if a window is opened. You may imagine that a magnet is hidden in the window sash (the moving part). A reed switch is buried in the frame so that the magnet is near it when the window is closed. Once the alarm sounds, it should continue even if the window is closed again; you will need to have a switch to reset the alarm.

Project   Automatic signal for a railway
Use a BISTABLE to make an automatic signal for a model railway. The train should turn the signal to red as it passes and then back to green when it has travelled some distance further. Two reed switch modules can be placed between the rails a suitable distance apart, and a small magnet can be taped underneath the last coach of the train.

Project   Fire alarm

Design a circuit which will sound an alarm if a fire occurs. Use a piece of fine copper wire or solder which would melt in a fire. When you test your circuit, cut the fine wire with scissors to pretend that it has melted.

Project   Light-controlled motor with emergency 'over-ride'

Build a circuit which will automatically turn off a motor when it gets dark. Include an emergency 'over-ride' switch (use an SPDT module) which can be used to keep the motor going even though it is dark.

Project   Car doors warning light

Build a circuit for a two-door car which will light a warning indicator on the dash-board if both doors are not properly shut.

Use two push-button switch modules to act as switches mounted in the doors, and an LED module as the warning light. The light should be on except when both switches are pressed.

Project   Daytime sleeper's doorbell

Suppose you work nightshifts and sleep all day. Build a circuit which will stop your doorbell ringing in the day when you are asleep, but will let it ring when it gets dark.

Use a push-button switch to act as the doorbell button, a buzzer to act as the bell, and an LDR to sense if it is day or night.

When you have built your circuit, change it so that the doorbell only sounds in the daytime and not at night.

Project   Night-time anti-theft device for cars

Build a circuit which makes it impossible to operate the starter motor of a car at night.

Use the motor module to act as the starter motor, and a push-button switch to act as the ignition switch.

Project   Seat-belt warning light

A car is to have a pressure switch inside the front passenger seat and a switch in the seat-belt mechanism which opens when the seat-belt has been fastened. Design a circuit which will show a red light if a passenger has not fastened the seat-belt, but a green light otherwise. (Remember that there may not be a passenger in the car.)

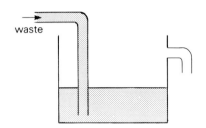

Project   Pollution warning system

A factory discharges waste liquid (which conducts electric current and which may be dirty) into a large tank with an overflow pipe. The waste is allowed to overflow into a river provided the liquid is clear.

Design a circuit which will sound a buzzer if the tank is full of dirty liquid.

Project   Night-time only latched burglar alarm

In Experiment 9.2 on page 68, you built a latched burglar alarm using the bistable circuit shown below.

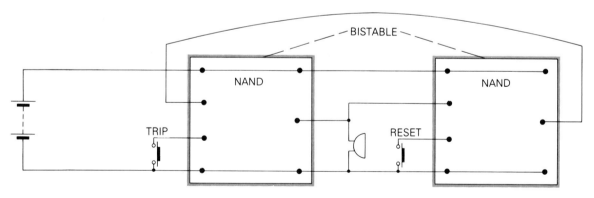

If the 'reset' switch is pressed, the buzzer is off. If the 'trip' switch is pressed, the alarm sounds and stays on until the householder presses the 'reset' switch again.

The problem of this project is to build a latched alarm that will work only in the dark. In the daytime, operating the trip switch should have no effect. At night, it should sound the alarm in the usual way.

Chapter 11 **Electronic control systems**

In most of the experiments and projects in this book, electronic circuits have been used to switch motors, LEDs and buzzers on and off. In other words, circuits have been used to control these devices. When electronic circuits are connected together to control things, the whole arrangement is called a control *system*. Systems are used, for example, to control what happens in aircraft, in power stations, in household appliances such as washing machines and microwave ovens, and for road traffic control and so on. Robots, operated by electronic control systems, are used nowadays, for example, in car factories. Electronic control systems are of ever-increasing importance in the world today, and much of the art of electronics lies in designing such systems.

This chapter looks at a simple control system in some detail to see how it might be built, first by using simple switches and then by using NAND circuits as the building bricks. There are not many experiments in it for you to do, but we hope you will read the chapter. It tells you how circuit diagrams can be simplified, and about logic circuits and how their truth tables can help in the design of a system.

Machines which make decisions

Suppose your parents ask that you should make them a pot of tea each day at 4.00 p.m. – if they want it. Then each day you have to make a series of decisions. Is it 4.00 p.m.? Is tea wanted? Is a teapot and tea available? Is there a kettle with water in it?

Each of these questions can be answered by 'yes' or 'no'.

If the answer to each of them is 'yes', then you would make the tea and tell your parents when it is ready. And since it would be a waste of time to make tea if it were not wanted, you need to know the best order in which to make your decisions.

The series of decisions can be shown by a flow chart:

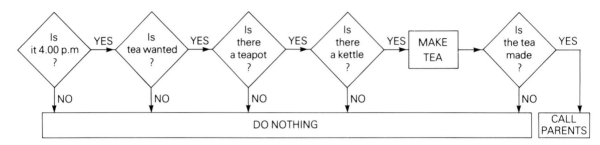

Of course you could make the decisions in another order – *you* can think for yourself. But suppose you decide to invent a machine to do this job for you. A *machine* cannot think for itself so the 'decisions' have to be in the right order. You may notice that each decision is like a switch. If the answer is 'yes', you go to the next question; if it is 'no', you do nothing. Here is an electrical equivalent of the flow chart:

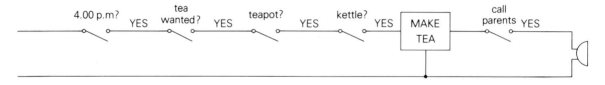

This electrical flow chart could form the basis of a machine. If an electricity supply were connected at one end, and if the first four answers were 'yes', the electricity could be connected to the heater in the kettle to boil the water.

Three other parts are needed besides the switches: a time-switch, a buzzer and a special 'tea-maker'. The time-switch is simply an electric clock which closes a switch at a set time, and keeps it closed for, say, half an hour. This is represented by the diagram on the left. (What would you have if you connected a buzzer between P and Q?) This time-switch will be the first switch in the electrical flow chart.

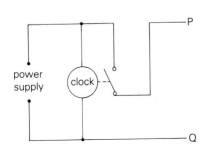

The most difficult part of the machine to invent is the part which makes the tea. The diagram below shows you how that can be done. The kettle part has a tightly fitting lid with a tiny hole in it and an electric heater inside. When the water boils, the steam cannot escape quickly and the extra pressure, which is caused by the steam, pushes the boiling water out through the tube into the teapot.

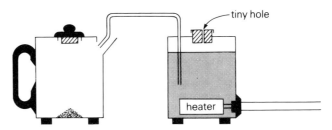

But the problem is not solved yet. The machine cannot *see* if the kettle has water in it or if the teapot is in the right place. This is why the decisions cannot be in any order. It would not do if the heater were switched on without the teapot in place or without water in the kettle!

To tell the machine whether the teapot is there and whether the kettle has water in it we need a pressure switch for each of them. The teapot and the kettle are on small platforms standing on short springs. A platform is pressed down when the teapot or the kettle full of water is in place. The springs supporting the kettle platform need to be stronger than those under the teapot platform because the kettle must not be able to press its platform down when it is empty. Each platform is fixed to an SPDT switch inside the base on which the platforms rest.

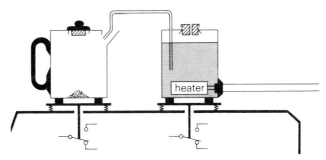

You may be worried about how the heater will be turned off when the tea has been made. If the electric current to the heater has to pass through the kettle switch, then, when the tea has been made and the kettle is nearly empty, the switch will change over and turn the heater off. And we can use the other contact of the switch to sound the alarm buzzer!

Now we can draw the circuit with its 'flow diagram' of switches.

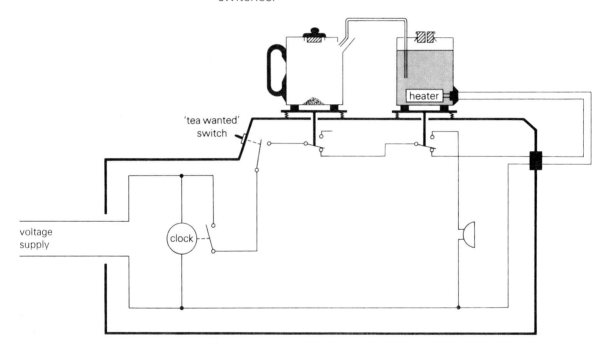

Logic circuits and circuit diagrams

What was described above was a *system* – a system of switches which allowed a useful job to be done. You may have noticed that the switches were in series, so forming an AND arrangement. That is to say, the electricity supply is only switched through to the heater if it is 4.00 p.m. AND tea is wanted AND the teapot is in place AND the kettle is there with water in it. In Experiment 7.4 on page 55 you found how to make an AND circuit using two NAND relay modules. So it should be possible to design a system for the automatic tea-maker using NAND modules.

The circuit diagrams in this book have used a special symbol for the NAND circuit. This was to help you to set up the circuits correctly. You will have noticed that drawing circuit diagrams became more difficult as the circuits became more complicated. The circuit diagrams became harder to understand and they took up more space as well. Some simpler way of showing circuits is necessary.

The diagram below shows an AND circuit.

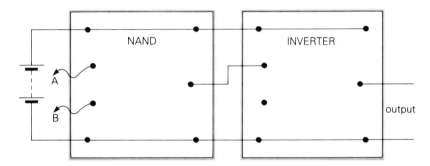

Obviously each module must be connected to the battery if it is to work. But we could leave the battery and supply rails out of our diagrams, provided we remembered that *all* the modules must be connected between the same supply rails. We must also remember that the input and output voltage levels are either HIGH or LOW *with respect to the negative supply rail*. The diagram now becomes:

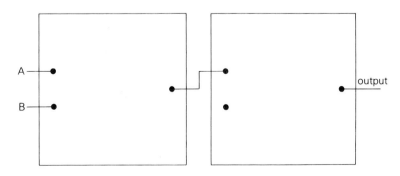

More space could be saved by using one symbol with two inputs and one output to represent these modules. The symbol usually used for an AND circuit is shown below, together with its truth table. The symbol is not hard to remember – it is like a D and AND ends with a D.

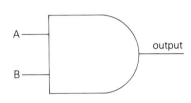

B	A	Output
0	0	0
0	1	0
1	0	0
1	1	1

That symbol can be used whenever it is not necessary to show that the AND circuit was made from two NAND circuits. But if we wish to show the two NAND circuits, we shall need to have symbols for them. The usual symbol for a NAND circuit is shown below, together with its truth table. The only difference from the symbol for the AND circuit is the small circle at the output. The small circle simply means that the AND output has been inverted. You can see that by comparing the two truth tables.

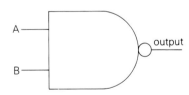

B	A	Output
0	0	1
0	1	1
1	0	1
1	1	0

How should an INVERTER be drawn? An INVERTER is a NAND module with only one input used. So it may be drawn like this:

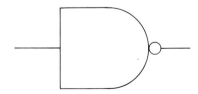

Thus:

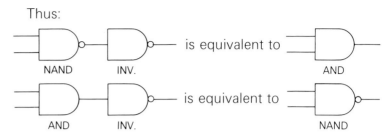

is equivalent to

Electronics uses circuits like AND, NAND and INVERTER circuits a great deal in designing systems. They are called logic circuits. They all have inputs and outputs. They are all switching circuits in which the voltage level of the output at any time depends on the voltage levels at the inputs. They are 'decision-making' circuits.

In addition to those logic circuits mentioned above, there are two more which are frequently used. These are the OR circuit and the NOR circuit.

The output of an OR circuit is high when either its A input OR its B input is high. The circuit symbol and the truth table for an OR circuit are:

B	A	Output
0	0	0
0	1	1
1	0	1
1	1	1

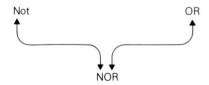

The output of a NOR circuit is Not high when either its A input OR its B input is high. The circuit symbol for it is the symbol for the OR circuit with a little circle at the output because it shows that its output is an OR circuit output inverted.

B	A	Output
0	0	1
0	1	0
1	0	0
1	1	0

It follows that:

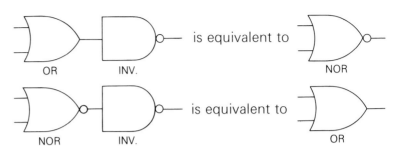

is equivalent to (OR + INV. → NOR)

is equivalent to (NOR + INV. → OR)

Combinations of circuits

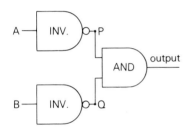

Circuits are often used in combinations, as shown in the example on the left. To help you understand how this circuit works, we have put the type of circuit inside the symbol though that is not usual with these diagrams.

To work out a truth table for this arrangement, it is necessary to build up a table which tells you what the voltage levels are at the intermediate points P and Q.

B	A	P	Q	Output
0	0			
0	1			
1	0			
1	1			

P is the output of an INVERTER, so that when input A is at a low level (0), P is at a high level (1), and vice versa. Copy the table and complete the P column.

Next, the Q column is the B column inverted.

Now that you know the P and Q voltage levels, you can fill in the output column because P and Q are connected to the inputs of the AND circuit.

If you have filled in the table correctly, you will find that the combination is a NOR circuit.

What sort of circuit is the combination shown on the left? You should find that it is an OR combination.

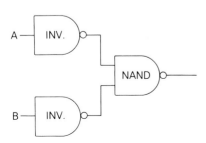

Using truth tables to design systems

The project problems at the end of Chapter 10 told you what the input and output devices were, but did not tell you about the circuits to use. Truth tables can help to solve the problem of which circuit to use when you are designing a system.

To show how this is done, take the the problem of the 'daytime sleeper's doorbell'.

The daytime sleeper's doorbell

a. The circuit has to prevent the bell from ringing during the day.

b. A push-button switch is to act as the doorbell switch.

c. An LDR is to sense whether it is night or day.

d. A buzzer can play the part of the bell.

The push-button switch is an input component and has to be connected between an input terminal and the negative supply rail. When the switch is open, the input is not connected and that means that it 'floats' HIGH. When the switch is closed, the input is LOW.

The LDR is the other input component. It is connected between an input and the negative supply rail. At night, its resistance will be large and it will act like an open switch and the input will float HIGH. In the daytime its resistance will be low and it will be like a closed switch, so that the input will be LOW.

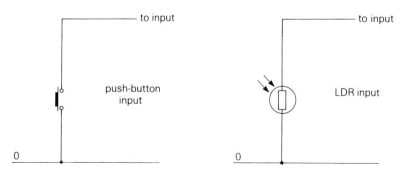

You want the buzzer to sound only when the door switch is pressed during the night. The buzzer will sound only when the output is HIGH. We can begin to make up a truth table:

Door switch	Time	Buzzer
open	day	silent
open	night	silent
closed	day	silent
closed	night	sound

which can be written

Switch Input B	Time Input A	Output
1	0	0
1	1	0
0	0	0
0	1	1

If you look at the truth tables on the previous pages or the summary in Appendix A on page 100, the only ones with outputs which have three '0's and a '1' are the AND circuit and the NOR circuit, but the inputs are different. Let us look at the AND circuit.

The AND circuit truth table:

B	A	Output
0	0	0
0	1	0
1	0	0
1	1	1

The truth table needed:

B	A	Output
1	0	0
1	1	0
0	0	0
0	1	1

How are these different? How do the B columns differ?

If the B column of the AND circuit truth table is inverted, we get the truth table needed.

So using an INVERTER on the B input (the doorbell switch) will produce a system which will do the job required.

The circuit is:

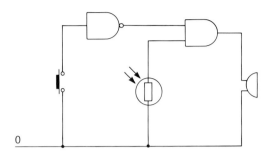

If only NAND circuits are used, the circuit is:

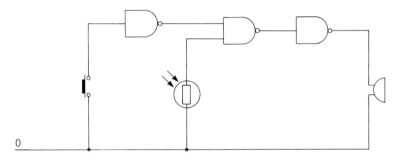

The automatic tea-maker again

It is possible to design the system for the automatic tea-maker using logic circuits. In that machine, the kettle heater was to be switched on only if each of the four switches were closed. Since a closed switch must connect an input to the low voltage level (remember that an open switch causes an input to float HIGH), the truth table for what is needed is:

Time?	Tea?	Teapot?	Kettle?	Heater
0	0	0	0	1 (on)
Anything other than the above				0 (off)

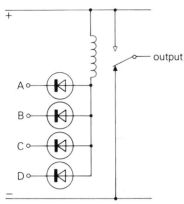

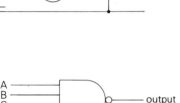

This time there are four inputs, and the circuits used for the experiments in this book have only two inputs! But there is nothing to prevent as many inputs as one wants being added to the NAND relay circuit, provided each has its own diode.

If any one or more of the inputs, shown on the left, is connected to the low voltage level, current will flow through the relay coil and that will switch the output to the high voltage level. Only if every one of the inputs is HIGH (or not connected) will there be no current through the coil and hence the output will be LOW. The truth table for this circuit would be:

A	B	C	D	Output
1	1	1	1	0
Anything other than that				1

Now compare this table with the one on page 87. All the inputs have to be inverted, and the output too. The output would have to switch the heater on by using a relay because the heater requires a lot of current. The circuit becomes:

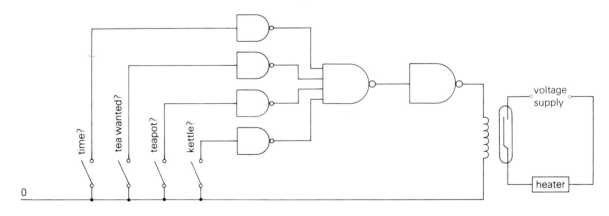

That leaves just the alarm buzzer to add. Remember that the buzzer has to sound when the tea has been made; that is to say, when the 'time', 'tea wanted' and 'teapot' switches are closed, but the 'kettle' switch is open. Another four-input NAND circuit and an INVERTER are needed to operate the buzzer. See if you can do it! (The answer is on page 111.)

This electronic system is more complicated than just four switches in series, but it has got some advantages. In the 'switches-only' circuit, the current for the heater from the mains supply has to pass through the switches. The switches have to be able to carry that current and be well enough insulated to protect the user from the dangers of the mains voltage supply. The NAND circuits work from much smaller voltages which are safe, and extra insulation is not needed. Indeed, except for the heater, the system could be operated from a battery.

But what about the expense of all the logic circuits? If the circuit 'building blocks' were NAND *relay* circuits, the system would be expensive without doubt. However a NAND circuit does *not* have to be based on a relay. Any circuit which has a NAND truth table could be used. NAND circuits can be made with transistors, and all the logic circuits for the 'automatic tea-maker' system could be manufactured on a piece of silicon about the size of a pinhead! This is what is commonly called a 'chip' and the chip for this system would cost less than 40p!

That is why electronics has become so important. Very complicated circuits can be made very small and very cheaply. No longer do you have to be a millionaire to own a computer.

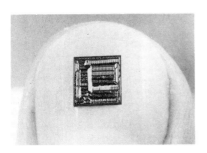

Background reading 1

Microelectronics and chips

From television, books and magazines, you have heard about microelectronics and the so-called 'chip'. What is microelectronics? What are chips? Why are they important?

Microelectronics is about very small electronic circuits. In the experiments you have been doing you have used a

NAND module, which was made with a relay, and it is quite large. In 1959 scientists found ways of making switching circuits such as NAND circuits in small, thin layers of silicon. This piece of silicon is known as a *chip*. It can be about the size of the nail of your little finger or even smaller.

The important thing was that several switching circuits could be made in the same chip. At first there were 10 or 20, but ways have now been found to make the switching circuits smaller and smaller, and today more than 100 000 can be put in a single piece of silicon only 5 mm square! These circuits can be connected together electrically inside the chip to make very complicated circuits. A magnified view of a silicon chip containing many circuits is shown in the photograph on the left.

Another name for a silicon chip containing many electronic circuits is an *integrated circuit* (or 'IC' for short). If you buy an integrated circuit, it will probably look something like the one shown below.

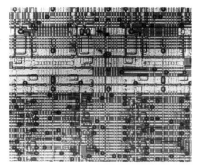

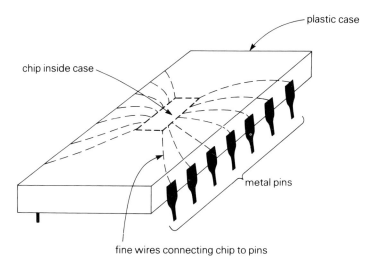

An example of a simple integrated circuit is the 'quad NAND' circuit. This contains four NAND circuits in a single silicon chip. The photograph shows such a chip and the diagram the connections to each NAND circuit.

As you can see, there are two pins to connect the positive and negative supply rails to the integrated circuit. The inputs and outputs of each of the four NAND circuits are brought out to separate pins. ICs like these are widely used and cost only a few pence.

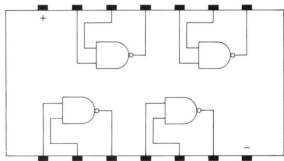

As well as being small and cheap, ICs are also very reliable and will continue to do the job for which they were made without trouble for a long time. The photograph below shows the ICs in a microcomputer. A few years ago a computer containing this number of circuits would have occupied most of a room; it would also have broken down often and would have cost hundreds of thousands of pounds!

Of course it is not just computers which contain integrated circuits. Nearly all electrical equipment, televisions, radios, washing machines, pocket calculators and so on, now contain 'the chip'. Its invention has revolutionised electronics.

Background reading 2

▲ user port

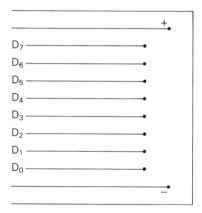

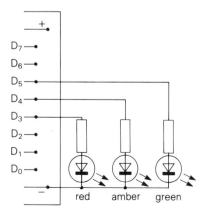

D7
D6
D5
D4
D3
D2
D1
D0

red   amber   green

Using a computer for control

Instead of using circuits such as NANDs or BISTABLEs for control purposes, it is also possible to use computers.

If you look carefully at most microcomputers, you will find that there is a socket, perhaps at the end, on one of the sides, or even underneath, called a 'user port'.

A port is somewhere where wires or conducting strips from the inside of the computer are brought to the outside. Most people working with computers use the word 'lines' to describe these conductors, so we shall do the same.

The number of lines brought to the user port is not the same for all computers, but in most it will be at least ten. Ten lines are shown in the diagram on the left. Two of the lines are the positive and negative supply lines from inside the computer (like the positive and negative supply rails in your electronics). The other lines (labelled D_0 to D_7) can be made HIGH or LOW by the computer in the same way that the output of a NAND module can be either HIGH or LOW. The important thing is that a series of instructions can be typed into a computer to tell it which lines to make HIGH and which LOW. This series is called a 'program'.

Suppose you wish to control a set of traffic lights. The first thing is to connect the three lights to three of the lines, as shown. A series of instructions must then be given to the computer to make the lights come on in the right order. The instructions must do something like the following:

1. Make line D_3 high, the others low.
2. Pause one minute.
3. Make lines D_3 and D_4 high, the others low.
4. Pause ten seconds.
5. Make line D_5 high, the others low.
6. Pause one minute.
7. Make line D_4 high, the others low.
8. Pause ten seconds.
9. Go back to instruction **1**.

When this program has been put into the computer, the instruction RUN is given and the program instructions will be carried out one by one in the order given. The lights will therefore come on and off automatically, and they will keep on doing so, since instruction **9** makes the computer go back to instruction **1** to keep repeating what happens.

Of course, with a real computer you cannot just type in the words shown above. You must use the programming language for the computer, which is described in the manual provided with the computer. You will find there are words in the programming language which make the lines go HIGH or LOW.

Another thing to know is that it is not a good idea to connect things like LEDs directly to the lines D_0 to D_7, as it is possible to damage the computer if wrong connections are made. It is usual to have a special 'interface box' between the computer and the outside world. This box usually contains special electronic circuits to protect the computer.

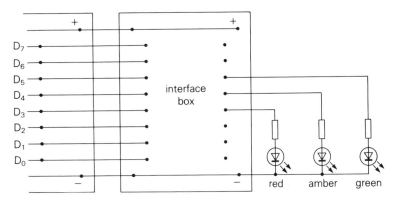

Other devices such as relays and motors can be connected to an interface box, and they can then be switched on and off using the computer lines.

You will have noticed that once again it is a matter of *switching* when working with computers like this, just as you were concerned all the time with switching when working with your electronic modules.

Chapter 12 **Yet more questions**

1. Write out the truth tables for (a) an INVERTER, (b) a NAND circuit, (c) an AND circuit, using 0 to stand for LOW and 1 for HIGH.

2. Complete the following statements:

a. If both the inputs of a NAND circuit are left unconnected, the output is ....

b. If only one input of a NAND circuit is used, and if that input is connected to the ... supply rail, the output is ....

c. A NAND circuit is so called because the output is ... only when ....

d. An AND circuit is so called because the output is ... only when ....

e. An OR circuit is so called because the output is high when ....

3. The diagram shows a bistable circuit in one of its stable states.

a. What effect does pressing switch P have? Explain your answer.

b. What effect does pressing switch Q have? Explain your answer.

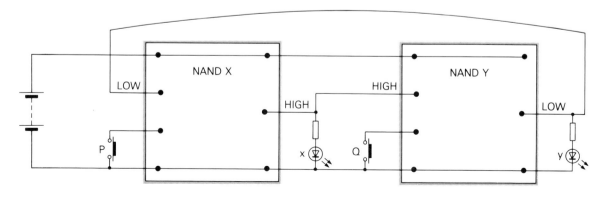

4. Copy the truth table and complete it for the circuit below.

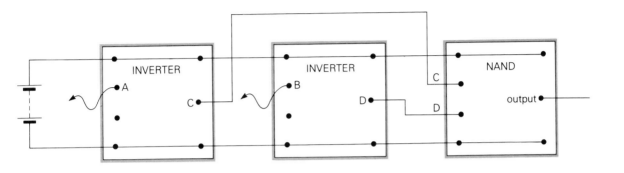

Input B	Input A	C	D	Output
0	0			
0	1			
1	0			
1	1			

a. In the column headed C, put down 0 or 1 for the output point marked C depending on what is written in the column headed A.

b. In the column D put 0 or 1 depending on what is in column B.

c. Use columns C and D to decide what should be in the output column.

d. What sort of circuit is this?

5. A thermistor is a special resistor whose resistance becomes smaller as it gets hotter. Draw circuit diagrams to show how it could be used to make a fire alarm using

a. a battery and a buzzer alone,

b. a battery, a buzzer and a reed relay,

c. a battery, a buzzer and a NAND circuit.

6. In the circuit below, what happens to the voltage levels at P and Q as the SPDT switch is moved from position 1 to position 2? How are the NAND circuits behaving?

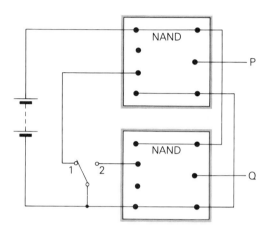

7. A student sets up the circuit shown below, with the switch S open.

a. What will the voltage levels be at each of the NAND circuit outputs A, B and C?

b. What do you think will happen when S is closed if each of the NAND circuits takes a little time to change?

(You might like to set this up and try it, perhaps using more NAND circuits. Comment on the number of NAND circuits you might use in the chain to get the effect.)

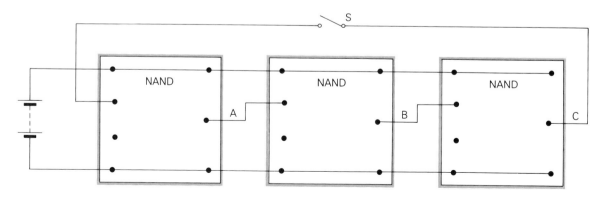

The remaining questions use abbreviated circuit diagrams as described in Chapter 11. You should draw circuits, where necessary in the following questions, in a similar way, using the correct symbols for any logic circuits you use and omitting the power supply rails and the battery.

8. Write down the truth table for each of the following circuits, which have their inputs connected together. Comment on your answers.

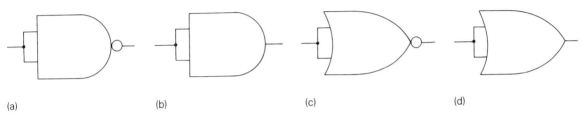

(a) (b) (c) (d)

9. Draw the circuits of questions **3** and **4** in their abbreviated form.

10. Using the NAND circuit as the 'building brick', draw the arrangement you would use for (a) an AND circuit, (b) an OR circuit, (c) a bistable circuit.

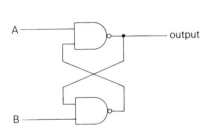

11. The circuit on the left appeared in a more advanced book about electronics.
a. What circuit is it?
b. Suppose the output of the circuit is HIGH. What would you do to make it LOW? Explain your answer.

12. In the following arrangement, inputs A and A' are left floating (not connected to anything). What will the output be if (a) input B is LOW, (b) input B is HIGH? Is this circuit of any use?

How would its behaviour differ if input A' were connected to the negative supply rail? Would it be of any use then?

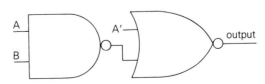

97

13. Logic circuits are often used in combination to form a system. In order to work out a truth table for the system, it is necessary to work out what the voltage level is at each intermediate connection for the various inputs. For example, if you want to know what happens at the output of the system below for different input levels at A and B, you must first find out what the voltage levels are at P and Q for the various inputs.

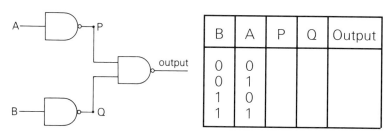

B	A	P	Q	Output
0	0			
0	1			
1	0			
1	1			

Copy the table and complete it. What sort of circuit is this combination?

14. Work out a truth table for each of the following combinations.

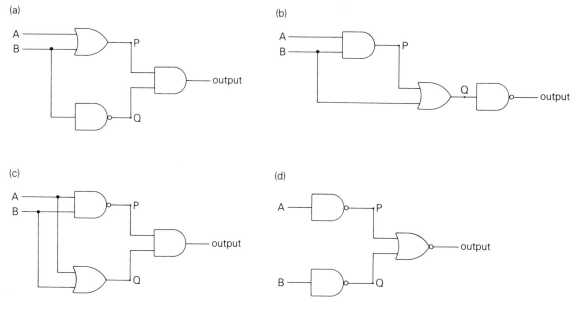

(a)

(b)

(c)

(d)

15. You have two push-button switches, A and B, a red LED, a green LED and a buzzer. Design a system, using logic circuits, which will cause the red LED to light if only A is pressed, the green to light if only B is pressed, and the buzzer to sound without the LEDs being lit if A and B are pressed together.

16. A student wishes to send out a message in morse using the circuit below. The idea is to flash the LED by means of the switch P, but it does not work.

a. Explain why it does not work.

b. What should be done in order to send out the message?

c. When another student sees the circuit, he remarks that the message 'passing through' the circuit is just like passing through a gate, with Q acting as a lock. What do you think he means?

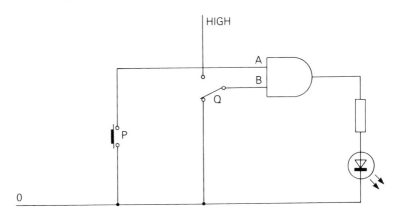

Appendix A **Summary of truth tables**

Electronics makes much use of logic circuits. These all have inputs and outputs, and they are all switching circuits in which the voltage level of the output at any instant depends on the voltage levels of the inputs. The various circuits may be summarised as follows. (A and B represent the two inputs, 0 represents connection to the LOW voltage level, 1 to the HIGH.)

AND

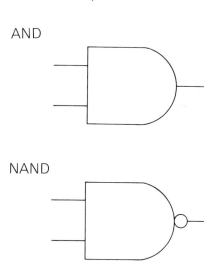

B	A	Output
0	0	0
0	1	0
1	0	0
1	1	1

NAND

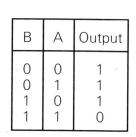

B	A	Output
0	0	1
0	1	1
1	0	1
1	1	0

OR

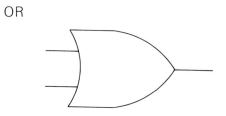

B	A	Output
0	0	0
0	1	1
1	0	1
1	1	1

NOR

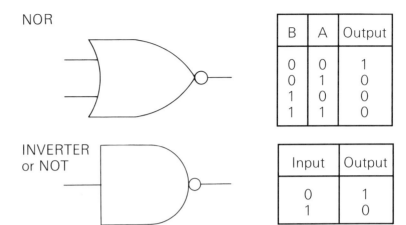

B	A	Output
0	0	1
0	1	0
1	0	0
1	1	0

INVERTER
or NOT

Input	Output
0	1
1	0

The INVERTER is sometimes called a NOT circuit for obvious reasons.

Appendix B **Solutions to projects**

In this appendix we have suggested possible solutions to some of the projects posed as problems elsewhere in the book. Of course these are not the only solutions; others will no doubt be suggested.

A current direction indicator (page 19)

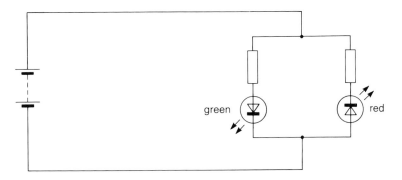

A very simple burglar alarm (page 21)

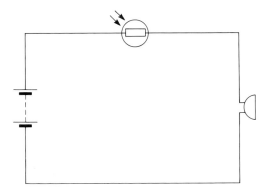

Manual control of 'stop–go' traffic lights
(page 29)

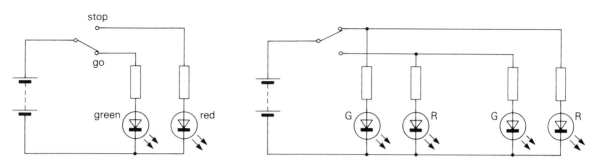

Staircase lighting (page 29)

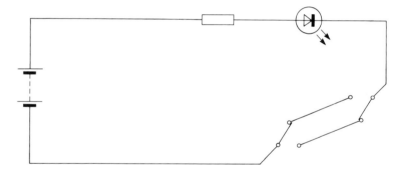

An automatically controlled washing line (page 33)

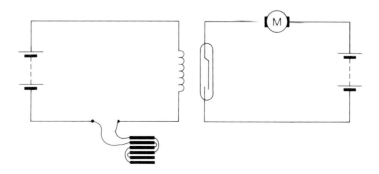

An automatic light (page 53)

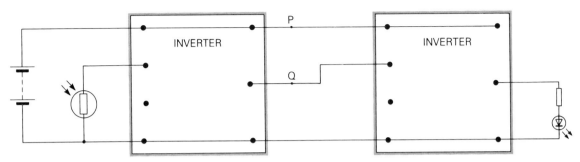

Note: the last INVERTER can be omitted if the LED is connected between P and Q.

A 'length' detector (page 55)

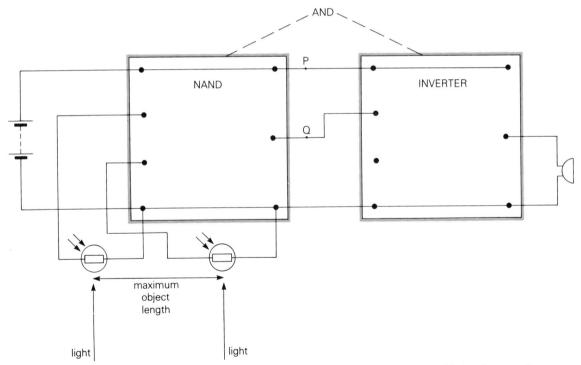

Note: the INVERTER can be omitted if the buzzer is connected between P and Q.

Teacher warning system (page 68)

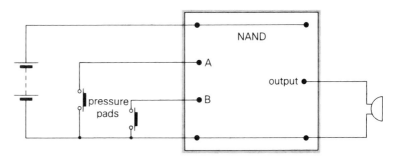

Controlling an electric motor (page 68)

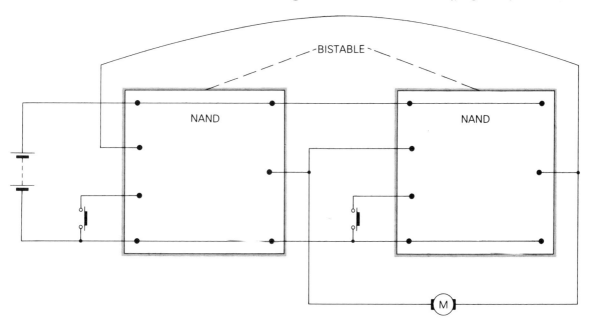

Vehicle moving backwards and forwards between light beams (page 72)

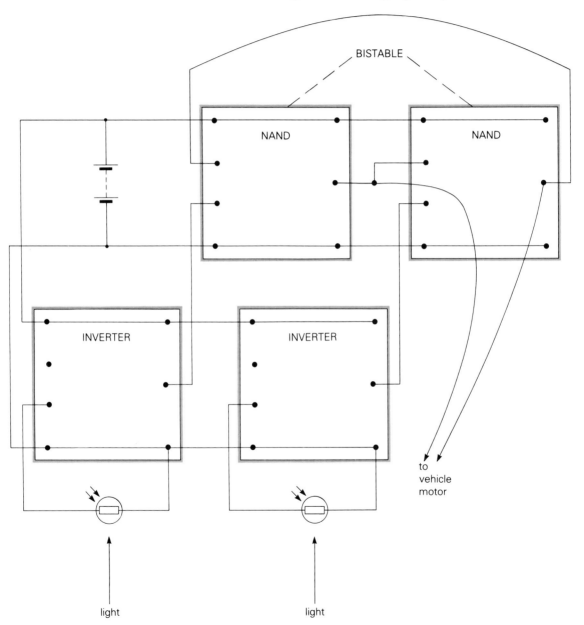

Window alarm (page 74)

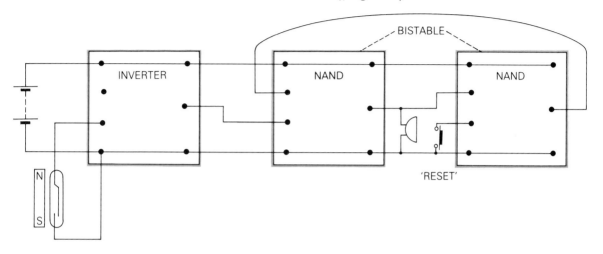

Automatic signal for a railway (page 74)

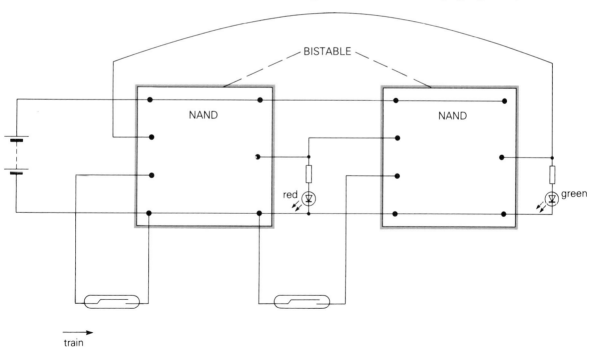

Fire alarm (page 75)

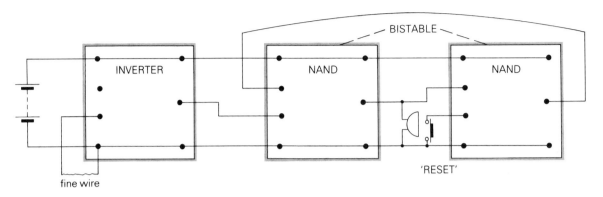

Light-controlled motor with emergency 'over-ride' (page 75)

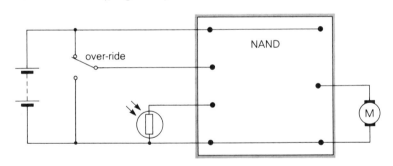

Car doors warning light (page 75)

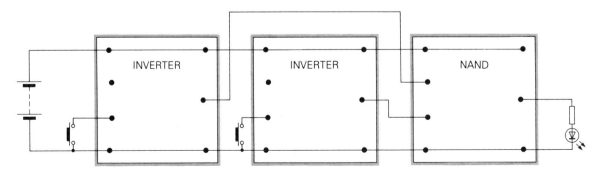

Daytime sleeper's doorbell (page 75)

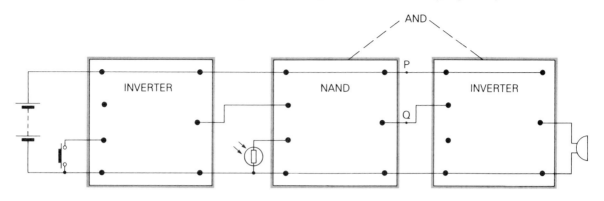

Note: the last INVERTER can be omitted if the buzzer is connected between P and Q.

Night-time anti-theft device for cars (page 75)

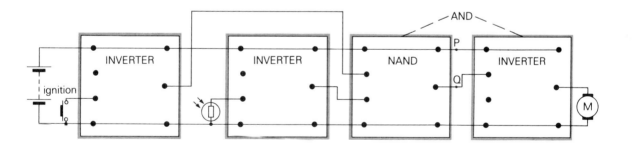

Note: the last INVERTER can be omitted if the motor is connected between P and Q.

Seat-belt warning light (page 76)

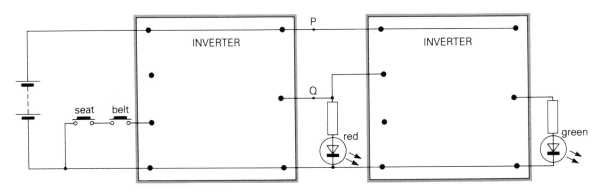

Note: the last INVERTER can be omitted if the green LED is connected between P and Q.

Pollution warning system (page 76)

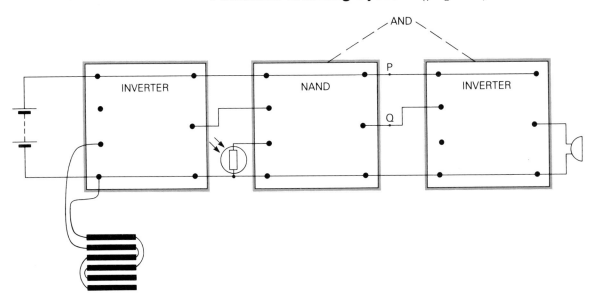

Note: the last INVERTER can be omitted if the buzzer is connected between P and Q.

Night-time only latched burglar alarm (page 76)

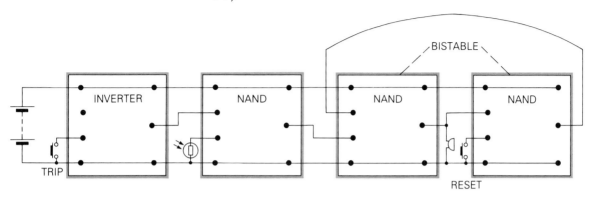

Circuit for automatic tea-maker plus alarm (page 88–89)

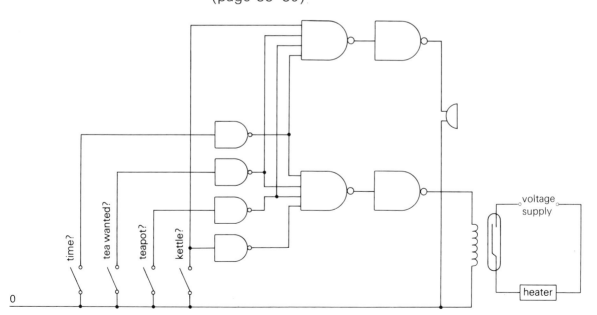

111

Index